Middle Credit Score® Fundamentals

The Plain-English Guide to How Mortgage Credit Really Works

Middle Credit Score® Fundamentals
The Plain-English Guide to How Mortgage Credit Really Works

This book is provided for **educational purposes only** and serves as the **official study guide for Middle Credit Score® Certification**.
It does not constitute legal, financial, lending, or credit advice, nor does it guarantee loan approval, loan terms, or credit outcomes.

Mortgage lending decisions are made by individual lenders based on their own underwriting guidelines, regulatory requirements, and risk assessments. Nothing in this book should be interpreted as an instruction to approve or deny credit.

Middle Credit Score® Fundamentals is designed to promote clarity, accuracy, and responsible education regarding mortgage credit evaluation. While every effort has been made to ensure accuracy at the time of publication, industry practices, regulations, and lender policies may change over time.

Published by:

Middle Credit Score®
United States of America

For educational resources and updates, visit:
MiddleCreditScore.com

ISBN: 979-8-9945570-1-3
First Edition
Printed in the United States of America

Contents

INTRODUCTION

Every year in the United States, **over 5 million mortgage approvals** are completed using a single credit score above all others.

Not the highest score.
Not the lowest score.

The **Middle Credit Score®**.

This has been the operational reality of mortgage lending for decades. Yet despite its widespread use, the framework behind this score remains poorly explained, inconsistently taught, and widely misunderstood by consumers and professionals alike.

Mortgage underwriting does not rely on opinions, estimates, or guesswork. It relies on structure, consistency, and risk evaluation. When three national credit bureaus produce three different scores for the same individual, the industry requires a reliable method to evaluate applicants fairly and consistently.

The Middle Credit Score® exists to serve that purpose.

This book defines the standard.

Middle Credit Score® Fundamentals documents the framework that governs millions of real mortgage decisions each year. It explains why the middle credit score exists, how it is used in underwriting, where it applies, and where it does not. It clarifies the difference between consumer-facing credit education and mortgage-specific credit evaluation, and it replaces assumption with structure.

This book does not introduce a new concept.
It defines an existing one.

The absence of a clear, authoritative explanation has created a gap in understanding across the industry. Consumers often focus on the wrong score at the wrong time. Professionals frequently rely on incomplete or generalized guidance. The result is confusion, misalignment, and avoidable financial consequences.

Middle Credit Score® Fundamentals exists to close that gap.

This is not a credit repair book.
It is not a collection of tactics, shortcuts, or strategies.
It is not theory.

It is the **foundational framework used in real underwriting decisions**.

Understanding the Middle Credit Score® is no longer optional for those operating in or around mortgage credit. As awareness increases, alignment becomes essential. Consumers benefit from clarity before outcomes are determined. Professionals require a common, verified foundation to ensure guidance is accurate, consistent, and responsible.

That is the purpose of **Middle Credit Score® Certification**.

Certification exists to establish trust through alignment. It ensures that those who advise, educate, or participate in mortgage transactions operate from the same verified understanding of how mortgage credit is evaluated. As this standard becomes more widely recognized, certification becomes the signal of clarity.

Lenders aligned with this framework demonstrate transparency and credibility. Certified professionals provide guidance rooted in structure, not assumption. Consumers gain confidence in knowing who understands the score that most often determines their mortgage outcome.

Middle Credit Score® is not a product.
It is not a trend.

It is a defined category within mortgage credit, and this book establishes its foundation.

For consumers, this book provides a clear explanation of the score most used in mortgage approvals, enabling informed decisions before applications are submitted.

For professionals, it establishes the baseline knowledge required to guide others responsibly.

For those pursuing certification, this book is foundational. All certification standards build upon the principles defined here, fundamentals, not exceptions.

This is how mortgage credit works.
This is the score behind millions of approvals every year.
This is the standard moving forward.

CERTIFICATION AUTHORITY PREFACE

The purpose of this book is not only to explain how mortgage credit works, but to establish a **standard, verified foundation** for those who educate, advise, or participate in mortgage-related decisions.

Mortgage credit decisions affect millions of consumers each year. When guidance is inconsistent, incomplete, or based on assumptions rather than structure, the consequences are real; financially, professionally, and systemically. For that reason, accuracy in how mortgage credit is understood and communicated is essential.

Middle Credit Score® Certification exists to establish alignment with the framework defined in this book.

Certification is not a designation of seniority, experience, or intent. It is a confirmation of understanding. It signifies that an individual or organization has demonstrated knowledge of how the Middle Credit Score® is used in real mortgage underwriting decisions and can accurately explain its role, limitations, and application.

As awareness of the Middle Credit Score® increases, so does the need for consistency. Consumers deserve clarity before outcomes are determined. Professionals require a shared language to ensure guidance is accurate and responsible. Lenders benefit when expectations are aligned, and education precedes transactions.

Certification serves as that alignment mechanism.

Those who complete Middle Credit Score® Certification are recognized for operating from the same verified framework outlined in **Middle Credit Score® Fundamentals**. This recognition allows consumers, professionals, and institutions to distinguish between opinion-based guidance and education grounded in established underwriting practice.

Certification does not replace lender discretion, underwriting guidelines, or regulatory requirements. It does not guarantee outcomes. It establishes credibility through demonstrated understanding.

As this standard continues to be adopted, certification will serve as a clear signal of trust, identifying those who understand the score that most often determines mortgage outcomes and who can communicate that understanding accurately and responsibly.

This book is the foundation for that standard.

Middle Credit Score® governs all certification criteria, continuing education requirements, and updates, and is subject to periodic review to reflect changes in industry practice, regulation, and credit evaluation methodology.

The chapters that follow define the framework upon which certification is based.

SECTION I — THE CORE TRUTH

Chapter 1:
What Is the Middle Credit Score®?

Quick Chapter Knowledge - Verification Framing
This chapter establishes the following conceptual understanding:

1. **Define** the Middle Credit Score® using an exam-accurate definition.

2. **Explain why** mortgage lending typically relies on three scores rather than one.

3. **Identify** the Middle Credit Score® when given three credit scores.

4. **Correctly communicate** the concept to a consumer in plain English without using confusing industry slang.

5. **Differentiate** between consumer-viewed credit scores and mortgage-underwriting credit scores.

6. **Recognize and correct** the most common misconceptions consumers hold about credit scores and mortgage outcomes.

Middle Credit Score® Fundamentals

What Is the Middle Credit Score®?

If you have ever checked your credit score, felt confident about where you stood, and then felt confused or surprised once the mortgage process began, you are not alone. This experience is incredibly common. Millions of homebuyers encounter this disconnect every year, often at the exact moment when clarity matters most.

That confusion is not the result of carelessness. It is not a failure to pay attention, prepare, or act responsibly. It happens because an important piece of the credit conversation is rarely explained clearly, if it is explained at all.

This book exists to fill that gap.

The Middle Credit Score® is one of the most important concepts in mortgage lending, yet it remains largely invisible to consumers until they are already deep into the process. It is not a new invention. It is not experimental. And it is certainly not a trick or loophole. It is a long-standing, widely used method that plays a central role in how residential mortgage credit is evaluated across the United States. For decades, mortgage lending has quietly and consistently relied on this approach. Borrowers were approved, denied, or priced using it every day, often without ever being told it existed. That silence created the confusion, not the method itself.

Once you understand what the Middle Credit Score® is and how it functions, much of the mystery surrounding mortgage credit begins to fall away. The process starts to feel less arbitrary. Decisions begin to make more sense. And the anxiety that often surrounds credit discussions is replaced with understanding.

This chapter is designed to introduce that clarity. It does not assume prior knowledge. It does not ask you to memorize rules or formulas. It simply explains, in plain language, what the Middle Credit Score® is and why it matters.

Everything that follows in this book builds on this foundation.

A Plain-English Definition

The Middle Credit Score® is exactly what it sounds like, but it is rarely explained that simply. When you apply for a mortgage, lenders do not look at a single credit score. They typically review **three separate credit scores**, each pulled from a different credit reporting system. These scores are collected simultaneously and reflect how your credit appears across multiple sources.

Once those three scores are obtained, they are placed in order from lowest to highest. The score that falls between the other two, the one that is neither the highest nor the lowest, is called the **Middle Credit Score®**.

That middle score is most often the score used to evaluate your mortgage application.

Not the highest score.
Not the lowest score.
The middle one.

This approach exists for a very practical reason. Credit data naturally varies across reporting systems. Timing differences, reporting cycles, and account updates can cause scores to move slightly out of alignment. Rather than reacting to those extremes, mortgage lending relies on the score that best represents the borrower's overall credit profile at that moment.

The Middle Credit Score® provides balance in a system where variation is expected. It does not exaggerate strengths or magnify weaknesses. Instead, it offers a stable, representative view of credit behavior, one that lenders can apply consistently and fairly across millions of applications.

Once this definition is clear, much of the confusion around mortgage credit begins to disappear.

Why You Have More Than One Credit Score

Many consumers are surprised to learn that they have more than one credit score. For years, most people have been introduced to credit through a single number often displayed by a bank, a credit card, or a credit-monitoring tool and labeled simply as "your credit score." It is easy to assume that this one number represents your entire credit profile.

In mortgage lending, however, credit is evaluated differently.

Mortgage lenders do not rely on a single score pulled from a single source. Instead, they review multiple credit scores to gain a more complete and reliable view of a borrower's credit behavior. This approach exists because credit information is not stored in one central location, and no single score can fully capture how credit looks across the entire system.

Each credit score reflects data collected from a different reporting source, updated on its own schedule. Because of that, variation is expected. One score may be slightly higher or lower than another, even when overall credit behavior is consistent. Mortgage lending was built with this reality in mind.

At this point, you do not need to understand all the mechanics behind why credit scores differ. That explanation comes later. What matters right now is understanding this foundational truth: having more than one credit score is normal, and mortgage lending is designed to work within that structure.

This book will walk you through the "why" step by step. For now, the key takeaway is simple—multiple scores exist, and mortgage lending already accounts for them.

Understanding the "Middle of Three"

A simple example makes this concept easy to see.

Imagine a borrower applies for a mortgage and receives the following three credit scores:

- 680
- 705
- 740

When these scores are placed in order from lowest to highest, they look like this:

- Lowest: 680
- Middle: 705
- Highest: 740

In this example, the **Middle Credit Score®** is **705**.
This does not mean the higher score is ignored, nor does it mean the lower score is being punished. It means the mortgage decision is anchored to the score that sits between the two extremes. That middle score provides a more balanced view of the borrower's credit profile, especially in a system where scores can vary slightly depending on timing and reporting.

By focusing on the middle score, mortgage lending reduces distortion.
It avoids overreacting to unusually high or unusually low data points and instead relies on a number that better represents overall credit behavior.
This approach creates consistency across decisions and fairness across borrowers.

Once the process is laid out this way, the concept itself is straightforward. What often confuses is not the method, but the fact that it is rarely explained before it becomes relevant.

Long-Standing and Standard Practice

One of the most important things to understand about the Middle Credit Score® is that it is not a workaround, a loophole, or a rule applied only in certain situations. It is a long-standing and widely accepted practice in residential mortgage lending.

This method has been in place for many years and is built directly into how mortgage credit is evaluated. It exists because mortgage lending requires decisions to be made consistently and predictably across a very large number of borrowers. When millions of loans are reviewed, the process must work the same way each time to be fair.

The Middle Credit Score® is not something lenders decide to use on a case-by-case basis. It is part of an established system designed to function at scale. By relying on a consistent method rather than subjective judgment, mortgage lending can evaluate borrowers using a framework that is stable, repeatable, and widely understood within the industry.

Understanding this helps remove another layer of doubt. The middle score is not an exception to the rules; it is part of the rules themselves.

Why the Score You See May Not Be the Score Used

Many consumers rely on credit scores provided by banks, credit card companies, or online credit-monitoring tools. These scores can be useful, and they serve an important purpose. They help people stay aware of their general credit health and notice changes over time. The confusion arises when those scores are assumed to apply to every lending situation.

The score you typically see is a single number, generated from a single data source and using a single scoring model. It reflects how your credit looks within that specific context. Mortgage lending, however, evaluates credit through a broader lens. Instead of relying on a single snapshot, it reviews multiple scores simultaneously to reduce the influence of timing differences, reporting gaps, or isolated fluctuations.

This difference in approach helps explain a common experience. A borrower may feel confident based on the score they see regularly, only to hear a different number discussed during a mortgage conversation. When that happens, it can feel like the rules have changed or that something was withheld. In reality, neither is true.

The discrepancy comes down to purpose, not deception. Consumer-facing credit tools are designed for monitoring. They provide a simplified view meant to keep people engaged and informed on a day-to-day basis. Mortgage credit evaluation, on the other hand, is designed for long-term lending decisions that involve greater risk, greater responsibility, and greater consistency.

Both approaches have value. They simply answer different questions. Understanding that distinction helps bridge the gap between what consumers see and how mortgage lending evaluates credit.

You're Not Behind, and You Were Never Taught This

If this is the first time you are hearing about the Middle Credit Score®, it does not mean you overlooked something or failed to prepare. It means this information was never clearly presented to you in the first place.

Most people are taught to "check your credit score" without being taught which score matters in specific situations, when it matters, or why it is used. That gap in understanding is built into the system. Credit education has focused on awareness, not application. As a result, many consumers move through the financial world doing exactly what they were told, monitoring a score without ever being shown how that score is used in mortgage lending. This is not a personal shortcoming. It is a structural one.

You are not behind.
You did not do anything wrong.
You were simply never given the full explanation.

This book is not here to correct your behavior or point out mistakes. It exists to clarify how the system works, so you can move forward with understanding rather than uncertainty.

What This Book Is and What It Is Not

This book is not a sales pitch. It is not written to steer you toward a specific lender, product, or financial decision. Its purpose is far simpler and far more important than that. It exists to explain how mortgage credit works; clearly, calmly, and without pressure so you can move through the process with understanding rather than uncertainty.

The goal is not to overwhelm you with technical rules, policy language, or insider terminology. Mortgage credit does not need to be complicated to be accurate. What most people have been missing is not intelligence or effort, but context. This book is designed to provide that context in an easy-to-follow, grounded way that reflects how lending decisions are truly made.

By the end of this chapter, you should understand one foundational truth: the **Middle Credit Score®** is the score most often used in mortgage lending, and it plays a central role in how applications are evaluated. Once that concept is clear, many of the frustrations and surprises people experience during the mortgage process begin to make sense.

Takeaways

- Mortgage lenders typically review **three credit scores**, not one
- The **Middle Credit Score®** is the score between the highest and the lowest
- This method is long-standing and standard in mortgage lending
- The score you see is not often the score used for a mortgage

This chapter defined the Middle Credit Score® and explained how it is derived from three credit scores used in mortgage lending. It established why the middle score is relied upon as a representative measure rather than the highest or lowest score.

The next chapter explains why three credit scores exist in the first place and how independent credit reporting creates variation.

Middle Credit Score® Fundamentals

"Key Definitions"

Middle Credit Score®
The credit score that falls between the highest and lowest of the three mortgage credit scores typically pulled at the same time for underwriting purposes.

Three-Bureau Score Set
A set of three credit scores produced from three separate national credit reporting systems, typically reviewed during the mortgage process.

Score Spread
The normal variation between a consumer's three mortgage credit scores. A score spread is expected and does not automatically indicate an error.

Mortgage Credit Score (Underwriting Score)
A score used in mortgage underwriting decisions, based on mortgage credit reporting methods and scoring models.

Consumer Credit Score (Monitoring Score)
A score a consumer views through a credit monitoring app or service; it may differ from mortgage underwriting scores and may create false confidence or unnecessary concern.

Underwriting Context
The principle that a credit score must be understood by *how it is used*, not merely what number it displays.

Middle Credit Score® Identification
The standardized method of determining the Middle Credit Score® by comparing the three credit scores pulled during a mortgage credit review and selecting the score that falls between the highest and the lowest.

Middle Credit Score® Language
The official vocabulary and standardized phrasing used to define, explain, and teach the Middle Credit Score® concept in a consistent and accurate way for consumers and professionals.

Middle Credit Score® Standard

The formal set of definitions, rules, and communication guidelines that governs the correct explanation and usage of the Middle Credit Score® concept, including how it is taught, referenced, and applied in certification materials.

Middle Credit Score® Fundamentals

"Foundational Evaluation Principles"

1. Mortgage lenders typically do **not** use a single score; they review **three**.

2. The Middle Credit Score® is the score **between** the highest and lowest score.

3. The Middle Credit Score® is a **standardized underwriting method**, not a loophole, trick, or consumer penalty.

4. The credit score a consumer sees most often is **not always** the score used in mortgage underwriting.

5. If a consumer is confused, it is typically due to **missing education and context**, not irresponsibility.

Middle Credit Score® Fundamentals

"Calculation Scenarios"

Scenario A:

Scores pulled: 612, 640, 663

☑ Middle Credit Score® = **640**

Scenario B:

Scores pulled: 701, 689, 735

☑ Middle Credit Score® = **701**

Scenario C (Same Score Tie):

Scores pulled: 680, 680, 712

☑ Middle Credit Score® = **680**

Scenario D (Low Outlier):

Scores pulled: 598, 661, 668

☑ Middle Credit Score® = **661**

Scenario E (High Outlier):

Scores pulled: 622, 646, 732

☑ Middle Credit Score® = **646**

Middle Credit Score® Fundamentals

"Standardized Explanatory Language"

☑ **1-Sentence Standard Explanation**

"In mortgage lending, three credit scores are usually pulled, and the score used most often is the one in the middle, not the highest or lowest."

☑ **Consumer-Friendly Explanation**

"You did not do anything wrong; mortgage lenders usually pull three scores, and they focus on the middle one as the most representative score for underwriting."

Middle Credit Score® Fundamentals

"Common Misconceptions"

Misconception #1: "My credit score is my credit score. There is only one."

☑ Correction: Mortgage lenders typically review **three credit scores**, not one.

Misconception #2: "The lender used the lowest score to punish me."

☑ Correction: The method uses the **middle score**, not the lowest.

Misconception #3: "If the scores are different, the report is wrong."

☑ Correction: Variation is expected. Different reporting systems create different scores.

Misconception #4: "Credit apps show the score lenders use."

☑ Correction: The score shown is often **not the score used** in mortgage lending.

Middle Credit Score® Fundamentals

Chapter 2:

Why Three Credit Scores Exist

Quick Chapter Knowledge - Verification Framing
This chapter establishes the following conceptual understanding:

1. Explain **why three credit scores exist.**

2. Identify the three main credit reporting organizations.

3. Explain why **data varies** between bureaus.

4. Describe why **score differences are normal.**

5. Explain why no bureau is "right" or "wrong".

Middle Credit Score® Fundamentals

Why Three Credit Scores Exist

Once people learn that mortgage lenders review more than one credit score, a natural question follows almost immediately: *Why are there three credit scores in the first place?* For many consumers, this realization can feel unsettling. It challenges a long-held assumption that credit is measured by a single, definitive number one score that follows you everywhere and means the same thing in every situation.

When different scores appear, it is easy to assume something is wrong. People often wonder whether an error has occurred, whether one score is "real" and the others are not, or whether the system itself is inconsistent. That reaction is understandable, especially when no one has explained why multiple scores exist in the first place.

The existence of three credit scores is not a mistake, a trick, or a flaw in the system. It is the result of how credit reporting developed over time, shaped by practical needs, independent data collection, and evolving financial markets, not by consumer education. The system was built to function, not necessarily to be intuitive.

This chapter is about removing that uncertainty. It explains where multiple credit scores come from, why differences between them are normal, and why none of them on their own tell the whole story. That clarity is the foundation for everything that follows.

The Role of Credit Reporting Organizations

In the United States, credit information is maintained by three primary credit reporting organizations:

- **Equifax**
- **Experian**
- **TransUnion**

These organizations play a very specific role in the credit system, and it is often misunderstood. They do not lend money. They do not approve or deny applications, nor do they make decisions about whether someone is a good or bad borrower. Their responsibility is limited to collecting, organizing, and maintaining information that creditors choose to report.

Each credit reporting organization operates independently. Every bureau maintains its own record of a consumer's credit activity based on the information it receives. There is no single. shared credit file that all three bureaus access or update together. This is one of the most important concepts to understand when it comes to credit scores, and it is rarely explained clearly.

This separation is not accidental. The system was intentionally designed to rely on independent records rather than a centralized source. Creditors are not required to report to all three bureaus, and when they do report, they may do so on different schedules. As a result, each bureau's record can look slightly different at any given moment, even when it reflects the same borrower.

Understanding this structure helps explain why multiple credit scores exist in the first place. When records are maintained independently, variation is a natural outcome. Different data leads to different calculations, which leads to different scores. That variation is not a sign of error or inconsistency; it is a byproduct of how the system was built to function.

Once this role is clear, the presence of multiple scores becomes less confusing. Instead of searching for a single "correct" number, consumers can start to see credit scores as interpretations drawn from separate but related records. That perspective is essential for understanding everything that follows in the mortgage process.

Why Credit Bureaus Do Not Share Data

A common assumption among consumers is that credit bureaus exchange information to keep their records aligned. On the surface, that assumption feels reasonable. If multiple organizations track the same type of information, it makes sense for them to share data to ensure consistency. In practice, however, that is not how the system works.

Each credit bureau operates independently. They are separate organizations with separate databases, and they do not merge or synchronize their records. Creditors, not the bureaus, decide where they report information. Some creditors choose to report to all three bureaus. Others report to only one or two. Those decisions are made for business and operational reasons, not because of consumer credit outcomes.

Because reporting is voluntary and selective, differences naturally emerge. One bureau may receive an update that another does not. One bureau may reflect a payment, balance change, or account update sooner, while another shows it later. Over time, these timing differences create variation across credit files, even when they describe the same borrower.

It is important to understand what these differences do *not* mean. They do not indicate that one bureau is more accurate, more trustworthy, or more legitimate than another. They also do not suggest that a consumer's credit is wrong. They simply reflect how information flows through a decentralized system.

The credit reporting system was never designed to produce identical records across all bureaus at every moment in time. It was designed to collect information from many sources and make it available for evaluation. Variation is not a failure of the system; it is a predictable outcome of how the system distributes and updates data.

Once this is understood, differences between credit reports stop feeling alarming. They begin to feel expected. And that understanding makes it easier to see why mortgage lenders evaluate credit using multiple sources rather than relying on a single, potentially incomplete record.

How Credit Reporting Works in Real Life

Credit reporting does not happen in real time, and it does not follow a single, universal schedule. Each creditor reports information based on its own internal systems, policies, and timelines. Payments, balances, and account updates are submitted in batches, often once per billing cycle, and those cycles can differ widely from one creditor to another.

Because of this, credit files are always slightly out of sync. A payment made this month might appear quickly on one credit report, show up later on another, and not appear at all on a third until the next reporting cycle runs. None of this means the payment was missed or ignored. It simply means the information has not reached every bureau at the same time.

From a consumer's perspective, this lag can feel inconsistent or even unsettling. It can create the impression that one report is "behind" or that another is more accurate. From the system's perspective, however, this behavior is normal. Credit reporting was built around periodic updates, not instant synchronization.

Mortgage lending learned to operate within this reality. Rather than relying on a single snapshot that might reflect incomplete or delayed information, the industry adopted a multi-record approach. Looking at multiple credit files reduces the impact of timing differences and provides a more complete picture of a borrower's credit behavior.

This approach acknowledges how credit reporting works in practice, not how it might work in theory. It accepts that data moves at different speeds and builds a decision-making process that accounts for that movement instead of being distorted by it.

Why Scores Can Differ Even When Credit Looks Similar

A credit score is not simply a list of accounts added up and averaged. It is a numerical interpretation of credit behavior, produced by a scoring formula that looks for patterns over time. Those patterns are shaped by details such as balances, payment history, and recent activity, all of which can change from one reporting cycle to the next.

Even when two credit reports look very similar at a glance, small differences can influence how a score is calculated. A balance update that appears on one report but not another, a payment that has posted in one system but is still pending in another, or recent activity that has not yet been reflected everywhere can all affect the outcome. These differences are often subtle, but scoring models are designed to respond to them.

It is also important to understand that scoring models are not measuring perfection. They are measuring risk patterns. They look at trends, consistency, and behavior over time, not just the presence or absence of individual accounts. Because each credit bureau's data may be slightly different at any given moment, the same scoring formula can produce different results depending on which data it is applied to.

This does not mean one score is correct and another is wrong. It means the system is interpreting similar information from slightly different points in time and context. The variation reflects timing and perspective, not error or inconsistency.
Once this is understood, score differences stop feeling mysterious. They become a normal and expected outcome of a system that relies on independently reported data.

For consumers with stable credit histories, variation in scores is not a warning sign; it simply reflects real-world credit activity.

Why Score Variation Is Normal and Expected

One of the most important truths about credit scoring is also one of the least clearly explained: **score variation is normal**. Having three different credit scores does not signal instability, inaccuracy, or unfair treatment. It signals that the system is functioning exactly as it was designed to function.

Credit scores are produced from independently maintained records, updated on different schedules, and interpreted through scoring models that respond to timing and context. When those elements are combined, variation is not an exception; it is the expected outcome. Differences between scores reflect perspective, not a problem.

Mortgage lending understands this reality. Score variation is not treated as something that needs to be corrected or eliminated. Instead, it is treated as a condition that must be managed thoughtfully and consistently. The process does not assume that one score tells the entire story. It assumes that multiple views are necessary to accurately understand a borrower.

Later chapters will explain how mortgage lending accounts for this variation in practice. For now, what matters most is recognizing that differences between scores are built into the system. They are anticipated, reviewed, and factored into decisions—not ignored or punished.

For many consumers, simply understanding this point brings immediate relief. Once variation is recognized as normal, the fear that something is "wrong" begins to fade. What once felt like uncertainty becomes a clearer picture of how credit works in the real world.

No Bureau Is "Right" or "Wrong"

Consumers often try to determine which credit bureau is the "correct" one. When scores differ, it feels natural to assume that one bureau must be accurate while another must be mistaken. That assumption, however, does not reflect how the credit system works.

There is no single bureau that holds the definitive version of a person's credit profile. Organizations such as **Equifax**, **Experian**, and **TransUnion** each maintain their own records based on the information they receive. Those records overlap, but they are not identical, and they are not intended to be.

Each bureau reflects the data that creditors choose to report to it, updated on that creditor's reporting schedule. Differences between bureaus usually come down to timing, scope, or reporting choices, not accuracy or bias. One bureau may show an update sooner. Another may still be waiting for the same information. Neither is wrong. They are simply reflecting different stages of the same underlying activity.

Mortgage lending does not attempt to decide which bureau is "best." Instead, it acknowledges that each provides a partial view. By reviewing multiple records, lenders avoid placing too much weight on any single version of the data. This approach recognizes that no single report captures the full picture on its own.

Understanding this removes another layer of unnecessary concern. When scores differ, it does not mean one bureau is working against you. It means the system is doing what it was designed to do: collect information independently and present it for evaluation from multiple perspectives.

Once that perspective is clear, the urge to chase the "right" bureau fades. What matters is not which record is superior, but how those records are evaluated together within the mortgage process.

How the System Evolved This Way

The credit reporting system did not appear fully formed, and it was never designed with today's consumers in mind. It developed gradually over decades, long before digital dashboards, mobile apps, or consumer-facing credit scores existed. In its early days, credit information was gathered locally, often by different organizations serving different regions, lenders, and industries.

As lending expanded and became more standardized, these organizations grew as well. Over time, they expanded nationally and began serving broader markets. Even as their reach increased, they remained independent entities, each collecting and maintaining credit information in its own way.
The system evolved to support lending decisions, not to explain itself to borrowers.

Mortgage lending did not redesign this system. It inherited it, rather than attempting to force a fragmented system into a single, unified record, mortgage lending adapted to the reality that multiple records would always exist. The use of multiple credit scores and, eventually, the reliance on the Middle Credit Score® emerged as practical responses to that structure. These methods allowed lenders to evaluate credit consistently without requiring changes to the underlying system.

Understanding this evolution helps explain why credit reporting looks the way it does today. What may seem inefficient or confusing from the outside is the result of layers of adaptation built over time. The system is not perfect, but it is functional, and mortgage lending learned to work within it rather than against it.

When viewed through that lens, the presence of multiple scores and the use of the middle score no longer feel arbitrary. They feel like solutions shaped by history, necessity, and scale.

Takeaways

• Three credit scores exist because credit data is collected independently by separate organizations
• Credit bureaus do not share data and receive updates on different schedules
• Score differences are a normal result of how credit information is reported
• No single credit bureau represents a definitive or complete credit record

This chapter explained why there are three credit scores and how independent credit reporting organizations collect and update data separately. It showed how timing differences, reporting choices, and decentralized data naturally lead to score variation.

The next chapter explains why mortgage lending relies on the middle score rather than the highest or lowest score.

Middle Credit Score® Fundamentals

"Key Definitions"

Credit Reporting Organization (Credit Bureau)

A company that collects, organizes, and maintains consumer credit information reported by creditors.

Equifax / Experian / TransUnion

The three primary credit reporting organizations used in the United States.

Independent Credit File

Each bureau maintains its own credit file. There is no single shared file that all bureaus update together.

Reporting Cycle / Reporting Schedule

The timing at which creditors send updated credit information to bureaus (not the same across all bureaus).

Score Variation

Differences in credit scores caused by timing, reporting scope, and data differences—not because the consumer did something wrong.

Middle Credit Score® Identification

A simple, repeatable way to determine which credit score is used most often in mortgage lending: compare the three scores and select the one in the middle.

Middle Credit Score® Language

The approved way to explain why three credit scores exist and why the middle score matters—using clear wording that reduces confusion for consumers.

Middle Credit Score® Fundamentals

"Foundational Evaluation Principles"

- The three bureaus **do not share or synchronize data.**

- Creditors are not required to report to all three bureaus and often report on different schedules.

- Score differences do not automatically mean "error." They are a predictable byproduct of the system.

- No bureau is "best," and no bureau holds the definitive record.

Middle Credit Score® Fundamentals

"Calculation Scenarios"

Scenario A: Different update timing
A consumer pays off a credit card. Experian updates first; Equifax updates later.
☑ Result: scores differ temporarily (normal).

Scenario B: Partial reporting
One creditor reports to TransUnion but not Equifax.
☑ Result: different credit file → different score (normal).

Scenario C: "Which bureau is correct?"
Consumer assumes the bureau with the highest score is the true score.
☑ Correction: no single bureau is "right."

Middle Credit Score® Fundamentals

"Standardized Explanatory Language"

☑ **Approved Explanation**
"You have three scores because there are three separate credit bureaus, and they do not share data. Each bureau updates at different times, so small score differences are normal."

☑ **Approved Explanation**

"Think of the three credit bureaus like three different cameras taking a picture of the same person; each angle captures something slightly different. That is why your scores can vary even when nothing is wrong."

Middle Credit Score® Fundamentals

"Common Misconceptions"

Confusion #1: "The bureaus should match exactly."
☑ Correction: They are not designed to match at every moment.

Confusion #2: "One bureau is inaccurate."
☑ Correction: differences usually come from timing/scope, not wrong data.

Confusion #3: "If my scores differ, I am at risk."
☑ Correction: score variation is normal and expected.

Middle Credit Score® Fundamentals

Chapter 3:

Why the Middle Score Is Used

Quick Chapter knowledge verification framing

This chapter establishes the following conceptual understanding:

1. Explain **why mortgage lending does not use the highest score.**

2. Explain **why mortgage lending does not use the lowest score.**

3. Explain why the **Middle Credit Score® is the "point of balance".**

4. Describe the role of the middle score in **fairness, predictability, and standardization.**

5. Communicate this concept confidently to a consumer in plain English.

Middle Credit Score® Fundamentals

Why the Middle Score Is Used

Once you understand that three credit scores exist and that differences between them are normal, the next question becomes unavoidable: *Why does mortgage lending rely on the middle score instead of the highest or the lowest?*

At first glance, the choice can seem arbitrary. Some consumers assume the middle score is used as a conservative measure, designed to protect lenders at the borrower's expense. Others believe it is simply a compromise, a way to split the difference that ends up disadvantaging people whose scores are spread apart. These interpretations are understandable, but they miss the larger picture.
The truth is more practical and far less personal.

The use of the Middle Credit Score® is not random or punitive. It was not adopted to make borrowing harder or to lower approvals quietly. It is a deliberate, time-honored choice to create balance in a system that must evaluate millions of borrowers using imperfect, real-world data.

Credit data is not static. It changes, updates, and flows through different reporting channels at different speeds. Scores reflect those movements, which is why variation exists in the first place. Mortgage lending needed a way to work within that reality without overreacting to short-term highs or short-term lows.

The middle score provides that stability.

By anchoring decisions to the score that falls between the two extremes, mortgage lending avoids relying on either the most optimistic or the most conservative snapshot. Instead, it evaluates borrowers based on a more representative view of their overall credit profile. This structure exists to apply the same evaluation method consistently across decisions and borrowers, resulting in predictable outcomes across the lending system.

Once this reasoning is understood, the selection of the middle score can be evaluated in light of its intended structural purpose. It begins to feel intentional. This clarifies how the middle score functions within a standardized mortgage evaluation.

Why the Highest Score Is Not Used

Many consumers naturally assume that the highest credit score should matter most. After all, it represents the borrower at their best. If one score is higher than the others, it seems logical to give it more weight. From a consumer's point of view, that expectation makes sense.

In large-scale mortgage lending, however, decisions cannot be built around best-case snapshots. The highest score often reflects the most favorable version of a borrower's credit profile at a specific moment in time. It may benefit from faster reporting, fewer accounts being reflected, or recent activity that has not yet appeared across all credit files. While none of this is wrong, it can create an incomplete picture.

Mortgage lending is designed to evaluate patterns, not peaks. A single high score can sometimes overstate credit strength if it is influenced by timing or temporary conditions rather than long-term behavior. When lenders rely too heavily on the most optimistic data point, outcomes become inconsistent, especially when comparing borrowers with similar histories but slightly different reporting timelines.

Consistency matters at scale. When millions of loans are evaluated each year, decisions must be based on methods that hold up across a wide range of credit profiles. Using the highest score would introduce too much variation. Two borrowers with nearly identical credit behavior could receive different outcomes simply because one bureau updated faster than another.

Mortgage lending is not built to reward the most favorable moment. It is built to assess sustainable risk over time. For that reason, relying on the highest score would undermine the goal of fairness and predictability and create uneven results across applications that should be treated similarly.

Understanding this helps clarify an important point: the highest score is not ignored because it is unimportant. It is not used because, on its own, it does not reliably represent the full picture that mortgage lending needs to see.

Why the Lowest Score Is Not Used

At the other end of the spectrum, it might seem reasonable to assume that the lowest credit score should matter most. After all, if a lender is managing risk, wouldn't it make sense to focus on the most conservative interpretation of a borrower's credit profile?

In practice, that approach creates just as many problems as relying on the highest score. The lowest score often reflects the most cautious snapshot of a borrower's credit file. It can be influenced by delayed updates, older account information, or reporting gaps that have not yet been resolved across all bureaus. In some cases, it may capture a moment in time that no longer accurately represents the borrower's current behavior.

If mortgage lenders relied solely on the lowest score, many borrowers would be evaluated more harshly than their overall credit history warrants. People with solid, consistent payment patterns could be penalized because one bureau lagged behind another. That would increase denials, introduce unnecessary friction into the lending process, and limit access to homeownership without meaningfully improving risk outcomes.

Mortgage lending is not designed to judge borrowers by their weakest moment. Just as evaluating best-case scenarios creates distortion, evaluating worst-case snapshots does the same. Both extremes exaggerate parts of the picture that were never meant to stand alone.

Using the lowest score would shift the system toward excessive conservatism, where caution outweighs accuracy. Over time, that would erode fairness and consistency, especially for borrowers whose credit behavior is stable but whose data updates unevenly.

This is why the lowest score is reviewed but not relied upon in isolation. It provides information, but it does not define the borrower. Mortgage lending requires a method that accounts for variation without allowing any single outlier, high or low, to dominate the decision.

The Middle Score as a Point of Balance

The Middle Credit Score® exists because neither extreme alone tells the full story. When credit data varies, as it naturally does, relying on a single high or low point can distort how a borrower is evaluated. Mortgage lending needed an approach that could account for variation without allowing any single data point to dominate the outcome.

By anchoring decisions to the score that falls between the highest and lowest, the system achieves balance. The middle score reduces the influence of outliers while still reflecting the borrower's overall credit behavior. It does not ignore strong performance, nor does it fixate on isolated weaknesses. Instead, it places them in context.

This approach is built on a simple and practical truth: when information comes from multiple sources and does not always align perfectly, the most reliable signal is often found between the extremes. The middle score functions as a stabilizer. It smooths timing differences, reporting gaps, and short-term fluctuations that would otherwise introduce inconsistency into the decision-making process.

Importantly, this is not compromised for the sake of convenience. It is not a shortcut or arbitrary. It is a deliberate design choice that allows mortgage lending to function fairly and predictably at scale. By using the middle score, lenders evaluate borrowers based on a credit representation that is grounded, repeatable, and consistent across millions of applications.

Once this role is understood, the middle score no longer feels like a concession. It feels like what it is: a thoughtful solution to a complex, real-world problem.

Risk Management in Human Terms

Risk management can sound abstract or technical, but at its core, it is really about predictability. Mortgage lending involves long-term commitments that often span decades, and those commitments must be made using imperfect information. Credit data is incomplete, constantly changing, and reported by many independent sources, each on its own timeline.

Because of that reality, mortgage lending cannot rely on any single moment or single data point. Decisions must be based on methods that hold up over time, across different borrowers, and across different market conditions. Predictability is what allows the system to function fairly and consistently, even when the information feeding into it is not perfectly aligned.

The Middle Credit Score® plays an important role in managing that uncertainty. It helps smooth out timing differences, reporting gaps, and short-term fluctuations that naturally occur in credit data. Rather than reacting to every small change, it provides a stable reference point that lenders can use repeatedly and reliably.

In human terms, this means borrowers are evaluated based on their overall pattern of behavior, not on their best or worst moment. It recognizes that credit history is a story told over time, not a snapshot taken on a single day. By focusing on that broader pattern, mortgage lenders can make decisions that are both practical and fair, even within a complex and imperfect system.

Why Consistency Matters at Scale

Mortgage lending does not happen in isolation. It operates at a national scale, across thousands of lenders, countless local markets, and millions of borrower profiles every year. In a system this significant, slight differences in how decisions are made can quickly turn into enormous disparities in outcomes.

Without a consistent method for evaluating credit, lending decisions would rely too heavily on individual interpretation. One borrower might be evaluated differently simply because they applied in a different city, worked with a different lender, or entered the process at a slightly different time. That kind of variability undermines fairness and erodes confidence in the system as a whole.

The Middle Credit Score® helps solve that problem by introducing standardization. It creates a shared reference point that lenders can rely on, regardless of geography or institution. Borrowers with similar credit behavior are evaluated similarly, not because they are identical, but because the method used to assess them is consistent. Consistency does not mean inflexibility. It does not mean ignoring individual circumstances or treating people like numbers. It means applying the same framework across decisions so that outcomes are predictable and comparable. When borrowers understand that the same rules apply broadly, not selectively, trust begins to build.

At scale, consistency is not just operationally efficient; it is also a driver of innovation. It is foundational to fairness. When rules are applied uniformly, borrowers can engage with the process knowing the same standards are being applied to them as to everyone else. That shared understanding benefits lenders and borrowers alike, and it is one of the reasons the Middle Credit Score® has remained a cornerstone of mortgage lending for so long.

Alignment With Established Lending Frameworks

The use of the Middle Credit Score® did not emerge in isolation. It aligns naturally with long-standing residential lending frameworks that were built to operate in a world where credit data comes from multiple sources. Conventional mortgages, along with government-backed programs such as FHA, VA, and USDA loans, were never designed around a single consumer-facing score. They were designed to function within a multi-score credit environment from the start.

These frameworks recognize a practical reality: credit information is gathered, reported, and updated by different entities at different times. Rather than forcing that information into a single number, mortgage lending adopted methods that could work reliably within that variability. The Middle Credit Score® meets that need because it evaluates borrowers using a balanced view of their credit profile rather than relying on an extreme.

Organizations such as **Fannie Mae** and **Freddie Mac** help establish the structural standards that support this approach. Their role is not to elevate one credit bureau over another or to prioritize a specific score. Instead, they provide consistency across the mortgage ecosystem, enabling lenders, borrowers, and markets to operate within a shared framework.

Within that structure, the Middle Credit Score® serves a clear purpose. It reflects balance rather than optimism or caution alone. It allows lending programs to evaluate borrowers using a method that is repeatable, predictable, and fair across a wide range of situations. Because of that, it fits seamlessly into the systems that have governed residential lending for decades.

Understanding this alignment helps remove another layer of doubt. The middle score is not an informal workaround or a lender preference. It is embedded in the way modern mortgage lending was built to function practically, consistently, and at scale.

Predictability, Fairness, and Standardization

At its core, the Middle Credit Score® produces three outcomes that matter deeply in mortgage lending. These outcomes are not abstract ideas or marketing language. They are practical necessities in a system that must consistently and responsibly evaluate millions of borrowers.

- **Predictability**, because decisions are based on a repeatable method that lenders can apply across applications and over time. Borrowers are not evaluated differently simply because of timing differences or isolated data points.
- **Fairness**: No single outlier, high or low, is allowed to define the entire credit profile. Borrowers are evaluated based on a more representative view of their behavior, not on their best or worst moment.
- **Standardization**, because similar credit profiles are treated similarly, regardless of where a borrower applies or which lender they work with. This creates a shared framework that supports trust across the system.

These outcomes did not happen by accident. They are the reason this method has endured. In an environment where data is imperfect and constantly changing, mortgage lending needed an approach that could balance variation without introducing bias or inconsistency. The Middle Credit Score® solved that problem in a scalable way.

When borrowers understand this, the middle score stops feeling arbitrary or impersonal. It begins to feel logical. More importantly, it begins to feel fair. What once looked like an unexplained rule reveals itself as a system built not to work against borrowers, but to work across them, consistently and predictably.

Takeaways

- Mortgage lending does not rely on the highest or lowest credit score because both extremes can distort a borrower's true credit profile.

- The Middle Credit Score® exists to balance variation, manage risk, and create consistency across millions of loan decisions.
- By focusing on the score between the extremes, lenders reduce the influence of outliers and evaluate borrowers more fairly.
- This approach aligns with established residential lending frameworks and has endured because it works.

This chapter explained why mortgage lending relies on the Middle Credit Score® rather than the highest or lowest score. It showed how using the middle score balances data variation, reduces distortion from outliers and supports consistent decision-making at scale.

The next chapter explains why consumers are often confused by mortgage credit and how gaps in education contributed to that confusion.

Middle Credit Score® Fundamentals

"Key Definitions"

Middle Score

The credit score between the highest and lowest of the three bureau scores used in mortgage evaluation.

Outlier Score

A credit score that is unusually high or unusually low due to reporting timing, missing accounts, or bureau update differences.

Point of Balance

The concept that the middle score is the most stable representation because it avoids reliance on either extreme.

Predictability

A repeatable method of evaluation that produces consistent outcomes across borrowers and time.

Fairness

A lending principle where one unusually high or low score is not allowed to define a borrower's entire credit profile.

Standardization

The application of consistent rules across the lending ecosystem so borrowers with similar profiles are treated similarly.

Middle Credit Score® Fundamentals

"Foundational Evaluation Principles"

- Mortgage lending evaluates **patterns, not peaks**

- The **highest score is not used** because it may reflect a best-case snapshot that is not consistent across bureaus

- The **lowest score is not used** because it may reflect a conservative snapshot influenced by delays, gaps, or outdated reporting

- The **Middle Credit Score® is used** because it stabilizes decision-making when credit data varies naturally between bureaus

- Middle-score usage exists to deliver:

    o **Predictability**
    o **Fairness**
    o **Standardization**

Middle Credit Score® Fundamentals

Calculation Scenarios

Scenario 1
Scores: **660 / 701 / 730**
☑ Middle Credit Score® = **701**

Scenario 2
Scores: **615 / 615 / 690**
☑ Middle Credit Score® = **615**
(When two are the same, the repeated value becomes the middle.)

Scenario 3
Scores: **580 / 640 / 742**
☑ Middle Credit Score® = **640**

Scenario 4
Scores: **720 / 721 / 722**
☑ Middle Credit Score® = **721**
(Shows why the system avoids "extremes.")

Scenario 5
Step 1 — List Each Borrower's 3 Scores

Husband's 3 Scores
- Experian: **682**
- Equifax: **710**
- TransUnion: **695**

☑ Sort them low to high: **682 / 695 / 710**

☑ Husband's **Middle Credit Score®** = 695

Wife's 3 Scores
- Experian: **658**
- Equifax: **640**
- TransUnion: **672**

☑ Sort them low to high: **640 / 658 / 672**

☑ Wife's **Middle Credit Score®** = 658

Step 2 — Select the Qualifying Score for the Loan

When there are **two borrowers**, the lender uses:

☑ **The lower of the two Middle Credit Scores®** (the "weaker middle")
- Husband's Middle Credit Score® = **695**
- Wife's Middle Credit Score® = **658**

☑ **Qualifying Middle Credit Score® used for the mortgage = 658**

Middle Credit Score® Fundamentals

"Standardized Explanatory Language"

☑ Approved Explanation

"The middle score is used because it is the most balanced and reliable. The highest score can be a best-case snapshot, and the lowest score can reflect delays or gaps, so lenders use the score between them to keep decisions fair, consistent, and predictable."

☑ Approved Explanation

"Mortgage lending does not use the highest or lowest score because those can be 'extreme' snapshots. The middle score is used because it is the most stable number when the bureaus do not match perfectly so borrowers are evaluated more consistently."

Middle Credit Score® Fundamentals

Common Misconceptions

Misconception #1: "They use the middle score to cheat consumers."
☑ Correction: It exists for **balance**, not punishment.

Misconception #2: "The highest score should always count."
☑ Correction: Mortgage lending avoids best-case snapshots because it creates inconsistency.

Misconception #3: "The lowest score should always count because lenders only care about risk."
☑ Correction: That would over-penalize borrowers and reduce fairness.

Misconception #4: "The middle score is just a compromise."
☑ Correction: It is a **repeatable system design** meant to stabilize outcomes.

Middle Credit Score® Fundamentals

Chapter 4:

Why Consumers Are Confused (And It's Not Their Fault)

Quick Chapter knowledge verification framing

This chapter establishes the following conceptual understanding:

1. Explain why consumer credit tools usually show only **one score.**

2. Explain why mortgage credit uses a **different system.**

3. Identify the **real cause of confusion** (education gap + marketing simplification).

4. Understand why consumer confusion is **not a personal failure.**

5. **Differentiate** between a "credit monitoring score" and a "mortgage underwriting score" (why they don't match).

6. **Describe** the most common false assumptions consumers make when they see a single score (ex: "this is the score lenders use").

7. **Explain** how to communicate the difference clearly and respectfully to reduce consumer fear, stress, and self-blame.

Middle Credit Score® Fundamentals

Why Consumers Are Confused (And It's Not Their Fault)

By this point in the book, you understand what the Middle Credit Score® is and why mortgage lending relies on it. You also understand why multiple credit scores exist and why differences between them are normal. Once those pieces fall into place, a quieter but more personal question tends to surface—one many readers feel but rarely say out loud:

If this system has existed for so long, why did not anyone explain it to me sooner?

That question is completely reasonable. It reflects curiosity, not failure. And the answer is not neglect, secrecy, or deception. It is rooted in how credit information has been presented to consumers over time, shaped by design choices that favored simplicity over completeness.

For decades, credit education focused on awareness rather than understanding. Consumers were encouraged to monitor, improve, and protect their scores, but were rarely taught how those scores would be used in real-world decisions. Mortgage lending, with its added layers and requirements, was treated as a separate conversation, one that often did not begin until much later in the process.

Over time, this separation created a gap. Credit information was widely available, but context was not. Assumptions filled the space where explanation should have been. Consumers assumed the score they saw was the score that mattered. Lenders assumed explanations could wait. Neither side was wrong, but the result was predictable confusion.

Understanding this gap is important because it removes self-blame. Confusion around mortgage credit is not a sign that you missed something or failed to prepare. It is a sign that education was incomplete. Once that becomes clear, frustration begins to fade, and clarity takes its place.

This chapter exists to make that distinction clear. It closes the loop between what you were shown and what was never explained. And in doing so, it allows you to move forward with understanding instead of doubt.

Why Consumer Credit Tools Show One Score

For most people, their first interaction with credit scores comes through familiar places, such as banks, credit card statements, or digital credit-monitoring tools. These tools are designed to be simple, accessible, and easy to use. To achieve that goal, they usually present credit information in the most streamlined way possible, which almost always means displaying a single score.

That single score serves an important purpose. It gives consumers a quick snapshot of their general credit health. It helps them notice trends, track improvement, and stay alert to major changes over time. In that context, simplicity is a strength. A single number is easier to understand, easier to remember, and easier to engage with regularly.

What that score is not meant to do, however, is represent every possible lending situation. It is not designed to account for the added complexity of mortgage lending, nor is it meant to prepare someone for the way credit is evaluated during a home purchase. It provides awareness, not precision.

The issue is not that these tools exist or that they show one score. The issue is that their limitations are rarely explained. Without that context, consumers naturally assume that the score they see is the score that matters everywhere. When they later enter the mortgage process and encounter a different conversation about credit, the disconnect feels confusing and unexpected.

Understanding why these tools show a single score and what that score is meant to do helps put the entire experience into perspective. It allows consumers to use credit-monitoring tools for what they do well, while recognizing that mortgage lending operates under a different set of expectations.

Why Those Tools Are Not Built for Mortgage Lending

Mortgage lending operates under a very different set of requirements than everyday consumer credit. A mortgage is not a short-term decision, and it is not based on a quick snapshot. It involves larger loan amounts, longer time horizons, and a responsibility that can span decades. Because of that, mortgage lenders are required to evaluate credit with more context, more data, and more consistency than most consumer credit situations demand.

Consumer credit tools were never designed for this level of evaluation. Their purpose is awareness, not underwriting. They help people keep an eye on general credit health, notice changes over time, and stay engaged with their financial profile. They are intentionally simplified so that consumers can use them easily and regularly without feeling overwhelmed.

These tools are not built to explain how mortgage lending works. They do not walk users through multi-bureau credit review, score variation, or standardized lending frameworks. They are not designed to prepare someone for a mortgage application, and they were never intended to replace education about how long-term lending decisions are made.

Expecting consumer credit tools to explain mortgage credit is like expecting a speedometer to explain how an engine works. Both are useful. Both provide important information. But they serve different purposes and answer different questions. One shows you how fast you are going. The other explains how the system functions.

When this distinction is not made clear, consumers assume that the information they see applies universally. When it does not, confusion follows. Understanding that these tools and mortgage lending serve different roles helps restore perspective. It allows consumers to appreciate the value of each without expecting one to do the other's job.

Both systems have value. They simply operate in different contexts, with different goals and different levels of complexity.

How Marketing Language Creates Misunderstanding

One of the most common sources of confusion around credit does not come from complexity—it comes from simplicity. Over the years, credit has been explained to consumers using language that is intentionally easy to understand and easy to repeat. Phrases like *"your credit score"* or *"check your score"* sound clear, approachable, and reassuring. They reduce friction and encourage engagement, which is exactly what marketing language is designed to do.

Over time, that language becomes familiar. It enters everyday conversation. People talk about their credit score as if it were a single, fixed number that follows them everywhere and applies to every situation. That belief feels reasonable because it has been reinforced consistently, often without qualification.

The issue is not that this language is misleading on purpose. The issue is that it is incomplete. Credit is not evaluated the same way in every context, and mortgage lending is one of the clearest examples of that difference. When consumers later enter the mortgage process and hear a different score discussed or hear multiple scores referenced, it can feel jarring. The natural reaction is to assume that something changed, or that new rules are suddenly being applied.

The reality is the rules did not change. The context did.

Consumer-facing credit language was designed to provide awareness, not precision. It offers a simplified view meant for general monitoring, not for long-term lending decisions. Mortgage lending, on the other hand, evaluates credit through a broader and more structured lens. When those two worlds collide without explanation, confusion fills the gap.

This is why so many borrowers feel caught off guard. They were taught to think about credit one way, and then asked to participate in a system that operates another way. Without reminding them that context matters, the shift feels unfair even though it is simply different.

Understanding this distinction is an important step forward. It allows consumers to see that nothing was hidden from them, and nothing was taken away. The conversation just moved into a different setting, one with different requirements and expectations.

Why Lenders Rarely Explain This Upfront

Many consumers reasonably wonder why mortgage lenders do not explain credit scoring, especially the use of multiple scores and the Middle Credit Score®, at the very beginning of the process. From the outside, it can feel like important information was withheld however, the explanation is far more structural than intentional.

Mortgage lending is a process-driven industry. Conversations often begin with goals, timelines, and basic qualifications, while deeper explanations are reserved for later stages. Lenders are trained to move borrowers through steps efficiently, assuming that detailed explanations can be layered in as needed. Unfortunately, that sequencing does not always serve consumers well.

In most cases, lenders operate under a few common assumptions:

- Consumers already have a general understanding of how credit works
- Detailed explanations can wait until an application is underway
- The mortgage process itself will provide enough context over time

These assumptions are rarely malicious, but they are often incorrect. Many consumers have never been taught how mortgage credit differs from everyday credit monitoring. When explanations are delayed, borrowers are left to fill in the gaps themselves, often with incomplete or inaccurate information.

Timing plays a critical role here. When credit is finally discussed in detail, it usually coincides with moments that carry emotional weight: an application review, a pre-approval decision, or a loan condition. At that point, the stakes feel higher. What could have been a calm, educational conversation earlier now feels urgent and stressful.

This is where confusion begins to compound. Borrowers may question their preparation, second-guess their decisions, or feel caught off guard by information they are hearing for the first time. The stress does not come from the credit system itself; it comes from learning about it too late.

It is essential to understand that no single lender, company, or professional creates this gap. It is the result of the mortgage system's evolution over time. Education was never formally built into the early stages of the process, so explanations became reactive rather than proactive. This book exists to change that sequence. By explaining how mortgage credit works *before* decisions are made, it removes pressure from the moment and replaces it with understanding.

How the Knowledge Gap Became Normalized

For many years, the credit system operated with very little consumer visibility. Credit decisions were mainly made behind the scenes, handled by institutions and professionals who understood the mechanics but rarely explained them. Borrowers were evaluated, approved, or declined, often without any clear explanation of *how* those decisions were reached. Education was not part of the process; it was assumed to be unnecessary.

As consumer-facing credit tools began to emerge, they were designed with good intentions. Their goal was accessibility. They made credit feel approachable and less intimidating by simplifying complex information into a single number or snapshot. This helped consumers stay aware of their general credit health, but it did not prepare them for mortgage lending, which operates under a different framework.

Over time, this created a quiet but significant disconnect:
- Consumers became familiar with *a* credit score
- Lenders continued to evaluate credit using *multiple* scores
- No clear explanation ever connected the two experiences

Because this disconnect was widespread, it gradually became normalized. Consumers came to expect confusion as part of the homebuying process. Hearing a different score during a mortgage conversation stopped feeling surprising and started feeling inevitable, even if it was never fully understood.

When confusion becomes common, it stops being questioned. Borrowers assume they missed something or failed to prepare appropriately. Stress becomes part of the experience, not because homebuying requires it, but because the system never provided clarity at the right time.

The most important thing to understand is that this normalization was not intentional. It was the byproduct of a system that prioritized efficiency and access over education. No one stepped in to slow the process down and explain the "why" behind the numbers. That does not mean this gap has to continue. With clear, plain-English education, the mystery disappears. What once felt confusing becomes understandable. And what once caused stress becomes something consumers can navigate with confidence.

How Confusion Compounds Stress During Homebuying

Homebuying is one of the most emotionally charged financial decisions most people will ever make. It involves timing, money, family, and long-term stability all at once. Even under the best circumstances, it carries weight. When credit feels unclear or unpredictable, that weight increases dramatically.

Uncertainty has a way of magnifying stress. When borrowers do not fully understand how their credit is being evaluated, every conversation can feel tense. Every update feels loaded. Instead of focusing on the excitement of moving forward, attention shifts inward. People begin questioning themselves rather than the system.

That internal questioning often sounds like this:

- "I thought I was ready."
- "Did I miss something important?"
- "Did I do something wrong?"

These thoughts are common and understandable. They arise not because borrowers failed to prepare, but because they were navigating a process without a clear map. When expectations are built around one understanding of credit and the reality turns out to be different, the emotional response is confusion, not confidence.

In most cases, the answer to those questions is no. Borrowers did not miss anything. They did not make a careless mistake. They did not misunderstand on their own. The confusion comes from a lack of clear, early education, not from a lack of effort, responsibility, or intelligence.

When people blame themselves for something they were never taught, stress becomes personal. That stress can overshadow good financial habits, solid preparation, and thoughtful decision-making. It can turn what should be a structured process into an emotional one.

This is why clarity matters. When borrowers understand how credit is evaluated *before* emotions run high, stress loses its grip. Confidence replaces doubt. Preparation feels validated instead of questioned. And homebuying becomes what it should be, a process you understand, not one you endure.

Takeaways

- Consumer credit tools typically show one score because they are designed for simplicity, not mortgage lending.
- Mortgage credit evaluation uses broader data and different methods, which are rarely explained early in the process.
- Marketing language reinforced the idea of a single score, while system assumptions perpetuated the knowledge gap.
- Over time, confusion became normalized, and stress became common.
- The misunderstanding was never personal; it was educational.

This chapter explained why mortgage lending relies on the Middle Credit Score® rather than the highest or lowest score. It showed how using the middle score balances data variation, reduces distortion from outliers, and supports consistent decision-making at scale.

The next chapter explains why consumers are often confused by mortgage credit and how gaps in education contributed to that confusion.

Middle Credit Score® Fundamentals

"Key Definitions"

Consumer Credit Tool / Credit Monitoring Tool: A platform built for awareness and trend tracking, not mortgage underwriting.

Single-Score Display: When a tool shows one score for simplicity and engagement.

Mortgage Credit Evaluation: A broader, stricter underwriting review requiring more context and consistency than consumer tools provide.

Knowledge Gap: Credit availability without credit context—leading consumers to assume the score they see is the score that matters.

Middle Credit Score® Fundamentals

"Foundational Evaluation Principles"

1. Consumer tools are meant for **awareness**, not mortgage precision.

2. Mortgage lending requires **multi-bureau context**, not a simplified "one number."

3. Confusion happens because the *system wasn't explained early*, not because the borrower did something wrong.

4. **A single score should never be treated as a mortgage decision score** (it's a monitoring reference, not an underwriting standard).

5. **Score differences do not automatically mean something is wrong**; they usually reflect different bureau data and update timing, not consumer failure.

Middle Credit Score® Fundamentals

"Calculation Scenarios"

Scenario A — The "One Score Trap"
- Consumer sees: **720**
- Mortgage pull produces 3 bureau scores (example): **690 / 706 / 732**
- **Middle Credit Score® = 706**

- Result: borrower feels blindsided even though nothing is "wrong"; they were never taught the system.

Scenario B — Why small differences are normal
- One bureau updates later.
- One creditor reports to only 1–2 bureaus.
- Score movement differs *even with the same consumer behavior.*

Middle Credit Score® Fundamentals

"Standardized Explanatory Language"

☑ Approved Explanation
"Most credit apps show one score because they are designed for simple monitoring, not mortgage approval. Mortgage lenders review all three bureau scores and then use the middle score for consistency."

☑ Approved Explanation
"Think of credit apps like a dashboard light; it gives a quick status, not a full diagnostic. Mortgage underwriting is the full diagnostic, and that is why they pull all three scores and use the middle one."

Middle Credit Score® Fundamentals

"Common Misconceptions"

- **"The score my bank shows is the score my lender uses."** (Not always.)

- **"If my mortgage score is lower, something changed."** (Usually the context changed, not the rule.)

- **"I should've known this already."** (No; education was incomplete.)

Middle Credit Score® Fundamentals

SECTION II — HOW MORTGAGE CREDIT ACTUALLY WORKS

5. How Mortgage Credit Is Pulled (Tri-Merge Explained)

6. Why Credit Scores Are Different (Score Spread Reality)

7. Where the Middle Credit Score® Is Used

8. Where the Middle Credit Score® Is Not Always Used

Chapter 5:

How Mortgage Credit Is Pulled (Tri-Merge Explained)

Quick Chapter knowledge verification framing

This chapter establishes the following conceptual understanding:

1. Explain what a **Tri-Merge Credit Report** is and why it is used in mortgage lending.

2. Describe what happens during a **mortgage credit pull** from start to finish.

3. Understand why mortgage credit pulls feel more serious than consumer credit checks.

4. Explain why a mortgage credit pull is a **structured confirmation step**, not a judgment.

5. Identify what lenders are really reviewing beyond the score (the "story behind the score").

Middle Credit Score® Fundamentals

How Mortgage Credit Is Pulled (Tri-Merge Explained)

For many borrowers, the moment credit is pulled for a mortgage feels different from any credit review they have experienced before. Even people who regularly monitor their scores or feel confident about their credit often describe this step with a mix of anticipation and unease. That reaction isn't a sign that something is wrong; it reflects the shift from credit as information to credit as part of a long-term decision.

Up to this point, credit may have existed in the background. It was something you checked periodically, tracked over time, or referenced casually. When a mortgage enters the picture, credit moves into a more formal role. It becomes one part of a broader evaluation that includes income, assets, and long-term affordability. That change in context, not the credit itself, is what alters how this step feels.

It is important to understand early on that a mortgage credit pull is not a judgment or a test. It is a snapshot. Lenders are not looking for perfection, nor are they searching for reasons to say no. They are gathering consistent information at a specific moment so decisions can be made responsibly and predictably. The process is designed to reduce uncertainty, not create it.

Mortgage credit is also not pulled casually or selectively. It follows a defined structure used across the industry, the same one applied to millions of borrowers each year. That structure exists to create uniformity, limit blind spots, and ensure that lending decisions are based on a complete view rather than a single data point. Nothing about this step is experimental or personal.

This chapter is here to remove the mystery before the mechanics appear. By understanding how mortgage credit is pulled and why it is done this way, you can approach the process with clarity instead of apprehension. Once expectations are aligned, what follows feels far more manageable and far less intimidating.

Orientation & Mental Model

For many people, the moment a mortgage credit check is pulled feels different from any credit check they have experienced before. Even borrowers who are confident in their credit often describe this step with a mix of anticipation and unease. That reaction is understandable. Mortgage credit pulls carry more weight, not because anything is wrong, but because this is where credit moves from abstract information to a real decision.

What is important to understand at the outset is that a mortgage credit pull is not a judgment. It is a snapshot. It is a structured way for lenders to see how credit appears across multiple sources at a specific moment in time. The goal is not to look for perfection or to catch mistakes. The goal is to gather consistent information so that decisions can be made fairly and responsibly.

This step often feels more serious because it represents a transition. Up to this point, credit may have been something you monitored, casually checked occasionally, tracked over time, or discussed in general terms. When a mortgage is involved, credit becomes part of a larger evaluation that includes income, assets, and long-term affordability. That shift in context is what changes the emotional tone, not the credit itself.

It also helps to know that this process follows a standard sequence. Mortgage credit is not pulled impulsively or without purpose. It happens at a defined stage, for a defined reason, and within a defined framework. Millions of borrowers move through this same step every year, using the same underlying process. Nothing about it is experimental or personal.

This chapter is here to remove the mystery before the mechanics appear. By the time credit is pulled, you should understand what the lender is doing and why. When expectations are clear, the process feels less intimidating and far more manageable. That understanding allows you to move forward with confidence rather than uncertainty.

What a Tri-Merge Credit Report Is

When people hear the term "tri-merge," it can sound technical or intimidating. In reality, the idea behind it is simple. A tri-merge credit report is a way to view your credit from multiple angles simultaneously, rather than relying on a single source.

In mortgage lending, credit information does not come from a single source. It exists across multiple reporting systems, each maintaining its own record. A tri-merge credit report combines those separate records into a single, unified view. It does not combine scores into a single number or average them. It simply allows lenders to see how your credit appears across all three sources at once.

The reason for doing this is consistency: credit data moves, updates, and changes on different schedules. One report might reflect an update slightly sooner than another. By reviewing all three together, lenders reduce the chance that a single delay or timing difference will distort the overall picture. The goal is not to favor one report over another, but to understand how they align.

What lenders are looking for in a tri-merge report is not perfection. They are looking for patterns. They want to see how credit behavior looks across multiple records over time, rather than reacting to a single data point that might sit unusually high or unusually low. Patterns provide context. Context creates reliability.

Seen this way, a tri-merge report is not about scrutiny; it is about perspective. It gives lenders a fuller, more balanced view of credit, enabling them to make decisions consistently and fairly. Understanding that purpose helps reduce much of the anxiety surrounding this step and prepares you for what comes next.

What Happens During a Mortgage Credit Pull

A mortgage credit pull usually happens after you have had an initial conversation, and you have permitted for your credit to be reviewed. This is important: lenders cannot simply "run your credit" without authorization. When it happens, it is not random. It is a planned step used to confirm where things stand so that the loan process can move forward with real numbers rather than guesses.

HOW MORTGAGE CREDIT IS PULLED (TRI-MERGE EXPLAINED)

What gets pulled is a mortgage-specific credit report that brings together the credit information lenders need to evaluate a long-term loan decision. It includes your credit history as it appears across multiple reporting sources, your credit scores from those sources, and the details that support those scores, things like open accounts, payment history, balances, limits, and any negative items that may be reporting. The lender isn't just looking at the score itself. They are looking at the story behind it, because the "why" matters as much as the number.

Here's the sequence in plain terms, without drama:

- **You authorize** the lender to pull mortgage credit.
- **The lender orders the report** through their system as part of the application or pre-approval process.
- **The report returns multiple scores and supporting credit file details**, organized in one place for consistent review.
- **The lender reviews the report** to confirm the qualifying score and to identify anything that needs clarification before moving forward.

From the borrower's perspective, this step can feel surprisingly quiet. You may not "see" anything happening other than a notice or alert from a credit-monitoring service. Sometimes people see a credit inquiry and assume something negative occurred. That inquiry is simply the footprint of the review. It's evidence that the lender looked at nothing more than that.

From the lender's perspective, this step is where uncertainty gets replaced with structure. It allows them to answer practical questions, such as: What score is being used for qualification? Does the credit file meet the program's required level of risk? Are there any obvious issues that should be addressed early to avoid stalling later? This is not about hunting for flaws. It's about confirming the facts, so the borrower is not surprised down the road.

The key takeaway is this: a mortgage credit pull is not a moment where you "pass" or "fail." It is the point where the lender shifts from assumptions to verified information. And once that information is clear, the rest of the process becomes more predictable for both sides.

Why Mortgage Credit Pulls Feel Different

Most people have had their credit checked before when opening a credit card, financing a car, or setting up a service. A mortgage credit pull feels different because the decision it supports is different. A mortgage is not a short-term transaction. It is a long-term commitment that often spans decades, and the credit review reflects that level of responsibility.

This step feels heavier because more is at stake. Homeownership carries emotional, financial, and personal significance, and credit becomes tied to something meaningful rather than transactional. When credit is connected to where you will live, how long you will stay, and what you will commit to over time, the process naturally feels more serious even if the credit itself hasn't changed.

Mortgage credit pulls are also more comprehensive by design. Unlike many consumer credit checks that focus on a narrow snapshot, mortgage lending looks at credit in a broader context. It reviews multiple records together, evaluates patterns instead of isolated moments, and uses that information to support decisions that must remain stable over the long term. That added scope is not about scrutiny; it is about reliability.

It is important to understand that this thoroughness is intentional, not punitive. The goal is not to find reasons to say no. The goal is to ensure that decisions are made carefully, consistently, and with enough information to protect both the borrower and the lending system. When credit is reviewed thoughtfully, it reduces surprises later in the process and helps prevent last-minute disruptions.

Recognizing why mortgage credit pulls feel different helps reframe the experience. The weight you feel is not a signal that something is wrong. It is simply the system doing what it was designed to do: slow down, look carefully, and make decisions that are meant to last.

Takeaways

- Mortgage credit is pulled using a tri-merge credit report
- All three credit bureaus are reviewed together
- Credit pulls are structured confirmation steps, not judgments
- The process is standardized across mortgage lending

This chapter explained how mortgage credit is pulled using a tri-merge credit report and why lenders review all three credit bureaus simultaneously. It clarified what information is evaluated during a mortgage credit pull and why this process is standardized across residential lending.

The next chapter explains why credit scores differ and how mortgage lending accounts for score variation without overreacting.

Middle Credit Score® Fundamentals

"Key Definitions"

Tri-Merge Credit Report

A mortgage credit report that presents a borrower's credit information from all three bureaus in one unified report so lenders can review the full credit profile consistently.

Mortgage Credit Pull

A lender-ordered credit review completed with borrower authorization to verify credit history, scores, and supporting details for mortgage qualification.

Authorization

The borrower's written or documented permission allowing the lender to order and review mortgage credit.

Credit Inquiry (Mortgage Inquiry)

The visible record that a lender reviewed credit during the mortgage process. It is the "footprint" of the review, not a negative event by itself.

Patterns vs. Perfection

A lending principle: lenders evaluate long-term behavior trends rather than expecting a flawless credit history.

Middle Credit Score® Fundamentals

"Foundational Evaluation Principles"

1. A mortgage credit pull is a **snapshot**, not a judgment.

2. Mortgage credit is pulled through a **structured, standardized sequence**, not casually.

3. A tri-merge report shows data from **all three bureaus at once** to reduce blind spots and timing distortions.

4. Lenders review more than the score; they review **the story behind the score** (accounts, payment history, balances, limits, derogatory items).

5. The goal of mortgage credit review is **consistency and predictability**, not perfection.

Middle Credit Score® Fundamentals

"Calculation Scenarios"

Scenario A — Identifying the Qualifying Score (Simple)
Tri-merge scores returned: **642 / 701 / 728**

☑ Middle Credit Score® = **701**

Scenario B — Tie Scenario
Tri-merge scores returned: **680 / 680 / 721**

☑ Middle Credit Score® = **680**

Scenario C — Why Tri-Merge matters (Timing Distortion)
A credit card balance updates on one bureau but not the others yet.
Scores returned: **614 / 663 / 668**

☑ Middle Credit Score® = **663**

(Shows why lenders view all three together instead of relying on one bureau.)

Middle Credit Score® Fundamentals

"Standardized Explanatory Language"

☑ Approved Explanation
"A mortgage credit pull is not a test you pass or fail; it is a verified snapshot. The lender orders a tri-merge report so they can review all three bureaus together and make decisions using consistent, complete information."

☑ Approved Explanation
"Think of a tri-merge report like a three-angle view of the same credit profile. It helps lenders avoid being misled by one bureau updating earlier or later than the others."

Middle Credit Score® Fundamentals

"Common Misconceptions"

Misconception #1: "If my credit gets pulled, it means something is wrong."

☑ Correction: Credit is pulled to replace uncertainty with verified information not to assume a problem.

Misconception #2: "Mortgage credit pulls are harsher than normal credit checks."

☑ Correction: They are more comprehensive, not harsher because the decision is long-term.

Misconception #3: "Tri-merge averages my scores into one number."

☑ Correction: Tri-merge combines the **reports**, not the scores. It displays multiple scores side-by-side.

Misconception #4: "The inquiry means my credit dropped and now my loan is in trouble."

☑ Correction: The inquiry is simply proof the lender reviewed credit, not a sign the loan is denied.

Middle Credit Score® Fundamentals

Chapter 6:

Why Credit Scores Are Different (Score Spread Reality)

Quick Chapter knowledge verification framing

This chapter establishes the following conceptual understanding:

1. Explain why credit scores from the three bureaus are **often different**.

2. Understand that score differences reflect **timing, categorization, and perspective**, not error.

3. Define what a **score spread** is in simple terms.

4. Identify common causes of credit score variation across bureaus.

5. Explain why mortgage lending expects score variation and uses the Middle Credit Score® to reduce distortion.

Middle Credit Score® Fundamentals

Why Credit Scores Are Different (Score Spread Reality)

By now, you understand that mortgage lending looks at more than one credit score and that the Middle Credit Score® plays a central role in how decisions are made. What often catches people off guard next is not which score is used, but the fact that the scores themselves are different.

That difference is often unexpected. When numbers do not match, it is natural to assume something is wrong, incomplete, or working against you. Many borrowers interpret score variation as inconsistency, instability, or even error, especially when no one explains why those differences exist in the first place.

This chapter exists to reset that assumption. Credit score differences are not a flaw in the system, and they are not a reflection of something you did wrong. They are a normal outcome of how credit data is collected, updated, and interpreted across multiple sources. Mortgage lenders expect this variation and are built to account for it.

Before discussing thresholds, outcomes, or pricing, it is essential to remove the anxiety around the score spread itself. Once the structural causes of score variation are understood, score differences can be interpreted without attribution or inference. They start to make sense.

Reframing the Surprise

For many people, the first time they see three different credit scores side by side, the reaction is immediate surprise. That reaction makes sense. Most consumers grow up believing there is one credit score that represents them everywhere, in every situation. When that expectation meets a different reality, it can feel unsettling, like something important has suddenly changed without warning.

The expectation of a single score did not come from nowhere. For years, credit has been presented to consumers as one number to watch, protect, and improve. That message is simple, easy to remember, and easy to engage with. Over time, it becomes natural to assume that this one number follows you consistently and tells the same story no matter where it appears.

Seeing multiple scores challenges that assumption. It raises questions that feel personal, even when they are not. People wonder whether one score is "right," whether another is "wrong," or whether the difference signals a problem they somehow missed. That reaction results from an expectation mismatch rather than from a problem with the credit data.

At the structural level, score variation does not indicate error or malfunction. Different credit scores are normal, expected, and already built into how mortgage lenders evaluate credit. Nothing went wrong when the numbers didn't match. You are simply seeing the system more clearly than you ever have before.

Why Score Differences Exist

Once the initial surprise fades, the next natural question is simple: *why are the scores different at all?* The answer is not complexity for its own sake, nor is it inconsistency in the system. Score differences exist because credit information is collected, updated, and interpreted independently rather than centrally.

Credit data does not live in one single place. It is gathered and maintained across separate systems, each receiving information from creditors on its own timeline. Because of that, no two credit records are ever perfectly synchronized. Even when the underlying credit behavior remains the same, the way it appears at a given moment can vary slightly depending on when the information was reported and how recently it was updated.

Timing plays a significant role. A payment, balance change, or account update might appear on one report quickly, appear on another a bit later, and lag on a third until the next reporting cycle. These are not errors. There are normal timing differences in how information flows through the credit ecosystem. When scores are calculated using data that is similar but not identical in timing, variation is a natural result.

Categorization also matters. Credit activity is organized into categories such as revolving accounts, installment loans, open accounts, and closed accounts. Slight differences in how an account is labeled, updated, or reflected at a given moment can influence how the overall credit profile is interpreted. These differences are usually subtle, but scoring systems are designed to respond to patterns rather than just raw totals.

Because of all this, "almost the same" data can still produce different scores. That does not mean the system is confused. It means it is responding to slightly different snapshots of the same credit behavior. The most common sources of variation include:

- Differences in when creditors report updates
- Variations in which accounts are present at a given moment
- Timing gaps between balance or payment updates
- How credit activity is categorized within each record

When you understand that score differences come from perspective and timing, not judgment or mistakes, the variation starts to make sense. What you are seeing is not instability. You are seeing a system designed to reflect real-world credit activity as it moves, updates, and evolves.

What a Score Spread Looks Like (Reality Check)

A **score spread** is simply the range between your lowest and highest credit scores at a given moment. That is it. It is not a diagnosis, a warning, or a signal that something is off. It is a description of how your credit appears across multiple records at the same point in time. Once you see it that way, the numbers can be evaluated descriptively rather than interpretively.

Here is a straightforward example of what a normal score spread can look like:

- **Lowest score:** 680
- **Middle score:** 705
- **Highest score:** 740

This range is standard. It does not suggest instability, risk, or inconsistency in your behavior. It reflects timing, reporting cycles, and perspective, nothing more. The scores are related, not conflicting. They are different views of the same underlying credit activity.

What often creates stress is not the spread itself, but the meaning people attach to it. A higher number can feel like a "true" reflection, while a lower number can feel like a setback when neither number tells the full story on its own. The spread exists because credit data moves in pieces, not because your credit is unpredictable.

This is why mortgage lending uses the Middle Credit Score® as a reference point between the extremes. The middle score sits between the extremes and serves as a reference point that reflects a more representative snapshot of the available data. When you understand what a score spread represents, the numbers stop feeling personal and start feeling informational.

Takeaways

• Credit score differences are normal and expected
• A score spread reflects timing and reporting variation, not risk
• Seeing multiple scores does not indicate an error or problem
• Mortgage lending is structured to account for score variation
• The Middle Credit Score® reduces distortion caused by extremes

This chapter explained why differences between credit scores occur and how score spread reflects timing, reporting variation, and perspective rather than instability. It clarified that mortgage lenders expect score variation and evaluate credit using methods designed to account for it.

The next chapter explains why credit history carries more weight than any single score and how lending evaluates patterns of behavior over time rather than individual moments.

Middle Credit Score® Fundamentals

"Key Definitions"

Score Spread

The range between a borrower's lowest and highest credit scores at a given moment.

Score Variation

Normal differences in credit scores across bureaus caused by timing, reporting, and data-category differences.

Timing Differences (Reporting Lag)

The delay between when credit activity occurs (payment, balance change, update) and when it appears on each bureau report.

Credit Categorization

How accounts are labeled and grouped (revolving, installment, open, closed), which can affect how scoring models interpret the same behavior.

Snapshot

A point-in-time view of a borrower's credit profile based on what each bureau shows at that moment.

Middle Credit Score® Fundamentals

"Foundational Evaluation Principles"

1. Credit score differences are **normal and expected**.

2. Score spread reflects **timing and reporting variation**, not risk by itself.

3. A score spread is descriptive, not diagnostic; it is not a warning.

4. Seeing multiple scores does **not** automatically indicate an error.

5. The Middle Credit Score® reduces distortion caused by extreme high/low outlier scores.

Middle Credit Score® Fundamentals

"Calculation Scenarios"

Scenario A — Identifying the Score Spread

Scores: **680 / 705 / 740**

- ☑ Lowest = 680
- ☑ Middle Credit Score® = 705
- ☑ Highest = 740
- ☑ **Score Spread = 740 – 680 = 60 points**

Scenario B — Small Spread (Typical)

Scores: **712 / 724 / 731**

- ☑ Middle Credit Score® = **724**
- ☑ Score Spread = **19 points**

Scenario C — Larger Spread (Still Can Be Normal)

Scores: **640 / 701 / 742**

- ☑ Middle Credit Score® = **701**
- ☑ Score Spread = **102 points**

(Does NOT automatically mean error — could be timing/reporting/categorization.)

Middle Credit Score® Fundamentals

"Standardized Explanatory Language"

☑ **Approved Explanation**

"It is normal to have three different credit scores. Each bureau updates on different timelines and may categorize information slightly differently, so your scores will not always match. The score spread is just the range — not a warning."

☑ **Approved Explanation**

"Your three credit scores are like three snapshots taken at slightly different times. If one bureau updates a payment or balance earlier than another, the scores can differ temporarily — and that is expected."

Middle Credit Score® Fundamentals

"Common Misconceptions"

Misconception #1: "If my scores are different, something is wrong."
☑ Correction: Differences are expected due to timing and reporting variation.

Misconception #2: "One bureau must be the 'correct' bureau."
☑ Correction: No bureau is automatically "right" or "wrong", each reflects a different snapshot.

Misconception #3: "A score spread means higher risk."
☑ Correction: A score spread reflects perspective and timing, not automatic risk.

Misconception #4: "The highest score is my true score."
☑ Correction: No single score tells the whole story; that is why the middle score is used.

Middle Credit Score® Fundamentals

Chapter 7:
Where the Middle Credit Score® Is Used

Quick Chapter knowledge verification framing
This chapter establishes the following conceptual understanding:

1. Explain why the Middle Credit Score® is a **dominant standard**, not a situational rule.

2. Understand mortgage lending as a **high-volume, standardized national system**.

3. Explain the scale of residential mortgage lending (approx. **5.6 million loans annually**).

4. Identify the major loan types where the Middle Credit Score® is standard (**Conventional, FHA, VA, USDA**).

5. Explain why consumers commonly misunderstand how often the Middle Credit Score® is used (visibility gap, not hidden rules).

Middle Credit Score® Fundamentals

Where the Middle Credit Score® Is Used

At this point, a reasonable question naturally emerges: *Is this really how most mortgages work?* When something isn't explained clearly or discussed openly, doubt fills the gap. Many borrowers assume the Middle Credit Score® is used only occasionally, selectively, or by certain lenders, simply because they've never been shown the bigger picture.

Mortgage lending, however, does not operate in isolated moments. It operates at scale. Millions of loans are completed every year under shared frameworks designed to produce consistent outcomes across markets, lenders, and economic cycles. Within systems that large, core standards don't drift quietly in and out of use.

This chapter exists to anchor understanding in reality, not opinion. By looking at mortgage lending through the lens of volume and structure, the role of the Middle Credit Score® becomes clear—not as a situational rule, but as a dominant standard. Before exploring exceptions or nuances, it's important to understand the baseline. This chapter establishes that baseline clearly and calmly.

Why This Question Matters

For many consumers, the idea that the Middle Credit Score® is used in most mortgage decisions feels counterintuitive. People often assume it applies only in certain situations, with certain lenders, or under specific circumstances. That assumption is understandable, especially when this method is rarely explained unless a borrower is already deep into the process. When something important operates quietly in the background, doubt fills the silence.

That doubt is reinforced by visibility or the lack of it. Consumers rarely see how mortgage decisions are made at scale. They see their own experience, a conversation with a lender, or a number displayed on a screen. What they don't see is the broader system operating consistently across millions of transactions. Without that context, it's easy to assume that the Middle Credit Score® is optional, situational, or applied inconsistently.

Clarity here matters because uncertainty creates unnecessary stress. When borrowers believe a key standard is applied "sometimes," they may second-guess outcomes, question fairness, or feel that rules change depending on whom they talk to. None of that reflects how residential mortgage lending works, but without a clear explanation, those assumptions persist.

This chapter exists to replace assumptions with perspective, not by arguing, persuading, or selling an idea but by grounding the conversation in reality. Before we talk about numbers, loan types, or institutions, it's important to understand *why* this question keeps coming up in the first place. Once that foundation is set, the answer becomes far easier to accept.

The Scale of Residential Mortgage Lending

To understand how standardized mortgage lending really is, it helps to step back and look at its sheer scale. Residential mortgages are not niche financial products or occasional transactions. They are among the largest and most systematized forms of consumer lending in the United States, operating continuously across every state, market cycle, and economic condition.

Each year, millions of households' complete mortgage transactions. These are not inquiries, pre-approvals, or applications that never go anywhere. These are finished loans, homes purchased, refinances completed, documents signed, and keys handed over. This volume includes first-time buyers, repeat buyers, homeowners refinancing, and families restructuring long-term debt. Mortgage lending touches nearly every demographic and income level in the country.

What matters here is not just the size of the number, but what that size implies. A system that supports millions of completed loans every year cannot function on improvisation or case-by-case judgment. It requires repeatable standards, shared definitions, and consistent processes that work the same way whether a loan is originated in a small town or a major metropolitan market—scale demands structure.

In plain terms, residential mortgage lending operates as a national system rather than a collection of isolated decisions. The rules governing credit review must hold up under enormous volume, diverse borrowers, and changing economic conditions. That reality is the backdrop for everything that follows in this chapter.

Headline context:

- Approximately **5.6 million residential mortgage loans** are completed annually in the United States
- This figure includes both **purchase and refinance** transactions
- These are **completed loans**, not applications or inquiries

Once you see mortgage lending at this scale, it becomes clear that the methods used within it must be common, standardized, and widely applied. That perspective sets the stage for understanding how credit evaluation fits into this system.

How Often the Middle Credit Score® Is Used

This is where the core question gets answered plainly, without hedging or qualifiers. In standard residential mortgage lending, the **Middle Credit Score®** is not used on an occasional or selective basis. It is used for the vast majority of the time. Once loans move beyond edge cases and into completed, guideline-driven mortgages, the middle score is the norm, not the exception.

Across the U.S. residential mortgage market, the Middle Credit Score® is used in **approximately 90% of completed loans**. That figure reflects how underwriting is performed in practice, not how it is perceived from the outside. When lenders follow established residential guidelines, credit decisions are anchored to the score that sits between the highest and lowest, not because it is convenient, but because it is consistent.

When that percentage is translated into real-world volume, the scale becomes easier to grasp. Out of roughly **5.6 million completed residential mortgages each year**, about **5.1 million** rely on the Middle Credit Score® as the qualifying score. These are not rare scenarios or specialized programs. They represent the everyday mortgage transactions that make up the backbone of the housing market.

These figures are intentionally rounded. The purpose here is clarity, not false precision. Mortgage volume fluctuates year to year, and exact counts vary with market conditions. What does not change is the proportion. Whether the market is expanding or contracting, the Middle Credit Score® remains the dominant standard for evaluating credit in residential lending.

Anchoring context:

- Approximately **90%** of completed residential mortgages use the **Middle Credit Score®**
- Roughly **5.1 million** out of **~5.6 million** completed loans annually
- Numbers are rounded to communicate scale, not to exaggerate

At this point, the takeaway is straightforward: if a mortgage follows standard residential lending guidelines, the Middle Credit Score® is almost always the score that matters.

Loan Types Where the Middle Credit Score® Is Standard

The reason the Middle Credit Score® is used so consistently is not a matter of preference or discretion—it is structure. Standard residential mortgage lending in the United States operates within established frameworks designed to function in a multi-score credit environment. Within those frameworks, the middle score is the qualifying reference point because it provides balance, consistency, and repeatability across millions of loans.

The Middle Credit Score® is standard across the most common residential loan types, including:

- **Conventional mortgages**
- **FHA loans**
- **VA loans**
- **USDA loans**

These programs account for the overwhelming majority of completed residential mortgages each year. While they differ in purpose, eligibility, and backing, they share a common need: a reliable way to evaluate credit when multiple scores exist. The middle score fulfils that role without relying on extremes, which is why it appears across programs with very different borrower profiles.

This standardization did not happen by accident. Institutions such as Fannie Mae and Freddie Mac help establish and reinforce consistent underwriting structures across the mortgage ecosystem. Their role is not to make individual credit decisions, but to ensure

72

that lenders across the country operate within a common foundational framework. The use of the Middle Credit Score® fits squarely within that mandate.

The core message here is simple and factual: **if a loan follows standard residential mortgage guidelines, the Middle Credit Score® is usually the qualifying score**. This is not an edge-case rule or a situational choice. It is embedded in the way mainstream mortgage lending operates. Understanding that removes the last layer of doubt about whether this method is common.

Why This Is Commonly Misunderstood

Even after seeing how widely the Middle Credit Score® is used, many people still carry a lingering sense of doubt. If this method is so common, the question naturally follows: *why didn't anyone explain it sooner?* That doubt is not skepticism; it is the byproduct of a system that operates largely out of view.

Most consumers believe the Middle Credit Score® is used "sometimes" because they encounter it only at certain points, often during a mortgage conversation. Until that point, credit is usually presented as a single number, consistently repeated across apps, statements, and marketing materials. When something new appears suddenly, especially something that matters, it feels like an exception rather than the norm.

The misunderstanding is rooted in visibility, not intention. Mortgage credit evaluation happens behind the scenes, and the mechanics are rarely discussed unless they become relevant. Lenders focus on moving the process forward, not on delivering a credit education lesson. As a result, borrowers experience the system's outcomes without ever being shown its structure.

It is important to be clear about what this does *not* mean. It does not mean there are hidden rules, shifting standards, or selective application. It means the system was built to function efficiently at scale, not to narrate itself along the way. Once the process is explained, the confusion tends to resolve quickly, not because anything changed, but because it finally became visible.

This is the point where doubt gives way to understanding. The Middle Credit Score® was never an occasional tool. It simply operated quietly, consistently, and out of sight until now.

Takeaways

- The Middle Credit Score® is not used occasionally; it is used in most residential mortgage decisions.
- Approximately 5.6 million residential mortgage loans are completed annually in the United States.
- Roughly 5.1 million of those loans, about 90%, use the Middle Credit Score® as the qualifying score.
- This standard applies across conventional, FHA, VA, and USDA mortgage programs.
- The belief that the Middle Credit Score® is used "sometimes" comes from a lack of visibility, not hidden rules or selective application.

This chapter established how frequently the Middle Credit Score® is used in residential mortgage lending and clarified that its application is the norm rather than the exception. It showed that the widespread use of the middle score is driven by scale, standardization, and consistency across major loan programs.

The next chapter explains the specific situations where the Middle Credit Score® is not always used and how those exceptions fit within clearly defined lending frameworks.

Middle Credit Score® Fundamentals

"Key Definitions"

Residential Mortgage Lending (National System)

A large-scale lending ecosystem that operates across all states using shared guidelines and standardized processes.

Standard Residential Mortgage Guidelines

Established underwriting frameworks used broadly across mortgage programs to ensure repeatable and consistent lending decisions.

Baseline Standard

The default method applied in mainstream mortgage lending before exceptions or edge cases are considered.

Qualifying Score

The credit score used by a mortgage lender to evaluate eligibility, underwriting, and pricing within standard guidelines.

Visibility Gap

When a standard process is widely used but poorly understood because it operates quietly in the background.

Middle Credit Score® Fundamentals

"Foundational Evaluation Principles"

1. Mortgage lending operates at scale, and scale requires **standardization**, not improvisation.

2. The Middle Credit Score® is used in the **vast majority** of standard residential mortgage lending.

3. Consumers often believe the Middle Credit Score® is used "sometimes" because it lacks visibility until it matters.

4. The Middle Credit Score® standard applies across major loan types (Conventional, FHA, VA, USDA).

5. Understanding frequency removes doubt: this is not a hidden rule — it is a common lending framework.

Middle Credit Score® Fundamentals

"Calculation Scenarios"

Scenario A — Understanding the Scale
If **5.6 million** mortgages are completed annually and ~**90%** use the Middle Credit Score®:

☑ Estimated loans using Middle Credit Score® = **5.1 million**

Scenario B — "Sometimes vs Most of the time"
A consumer assumes Middle Credit Score® is used occasionally.

☑ Reality check: In standard residential lending, it applies roughly **9 out of 10 loans**.

Scenario C — Loan Program Consistency
Borrower qualifies under FHA guidelines.

☑ Middle Credit Score® is still typically the qualifying score because FHA lending operates in the same multi-score environment.

Middle Credit Score® Fundamentals

"Standardized Explanatory Language"

☑ **Approved Explanation**
"The Middle Credit Score® is not used occasionally; it is used in most standard residential mortgages. Because mortgage lending happens at national scale, lenders rely on consistent guidelines, and the middle score is the common qualifying standard."

✅ **Approved Explanation**

"Mortgage lending is not a case-by-case system. It is a high-volume national system, and high-volume systems require repeatable rules. That is why the Middle Credit Score® is used across most mainstream loan programs."

Middle Credit Score® Fundamentals

"Common Misconceptions"

Misconception #1: "The Middle Credit Score® is only used by certain lenders."
✅ Correction: It is used broadly across standard residential lending.

Misconception #2: "If it was common, I would have heard of it sooner."
✅ Correction: It is misunderstood because the process operates quietly until a mortgage conversation begins.

Misconception #3: "The rules change depending on who you talk to."
✅ Correction: Standard·residential mortgage lending follows common frameworks designed for consistency.

Misconception #4: "It feels like a special rule because I only discovered it during the mortgage process."
✅ Correction: That is a visibility issue, not a selective application issue.

Middle Credit Score® Fundamentals

Chapter 8:

Where the Middle Credit Score® Is Not Always Used

Quick Chapter knowledge verification framing

This chapter establishes the following conceptual understanding:

1. Explain why credibility requires understanding **boundaries and exceptions**.

2. Understand that exceptions do **not weaken** the Middle Credit Score® framework.

3. Identify loan categories that may fall outside standard residential guidelines.

4. Explain why different loan structures require different evaluation methods.

5. Communicate the difference between **standard residential lending** and **specialized lending** without creating doubt.

Middle Credit Score® Fundamentals

Where the Middle Credit Score® Is Not Always Used

A framework is only credible if its boundaries are clearly defined. While the Middle Credit Score® plays a central role in standard residential mortgage lending, it is not used in every loan scenario and understanding that distinction matters.

Some borrowers assume that if a rule has exceptions, it must not be reliable when actually, the opposite is true. Well-designed systems apply consistently where intended, and they allow different methods when the loan structure changes. That flexibility is a sign of strength, not weakness.

This chapter exists to clarify those boundaries. Not to diminish the importance of the Middle Credit Score®, but to place it accurately within the broader lending landscape. When borrowers understand *where* a standard applies and *why* it does not apply elsewhere, confidence increases rather than erodes.

Clarity about exceptions prevents overgeneralization, misinformation, and unnecessary doubt. With that clarity in place, the role of the Middle Credit Score® becomes even more grounded and credible.

Why Exceptions Matter

Up to this point in the book, you've seen how consistently the Middle Credit Score® is used across standard residential mortgage lending. That consistency matters. But credibility requires something just as important as clarity: honesty about boundaries. No system that operates at a national scale applies in every single scenario without exception, and pretending otherwise would undermine everything you've learned so far.

This chapter exists not to weaken the role of the Middle Credit Score®, but to strengthen it. Understanding where a rule applies is only half of understanding how a system works. Knowing where it does *not* apply completes the picture. When boundaries are clearly defined, confidence increases, not decreases.

Many consumers assume that if something isn't used everywhere, it must not matter very much. That assumption feels logical, but it misunderstands how lending frameworks are built. Residential mortgage standards are designed around the most common, regulated, and repeatable loan types, not around niche or specialized products that operate outside those structures.

Recognizing exceptions is not about casting doubt. It is about accuracy. The Middle Credit Score® remains central to most residential mortgages precisely because it functions within standardized guidelines. Where those guidelines do not apply, different methods step in, not because the middle score failed, but because the loan itself follows a different set of rules.

Loans That Fall Outside Standard Residential Guidelines

While most residential mortgages follow standardized frameworks, some loans are intentionally designed to operate outside those boundaries. These products exist to serve borrowers or situations that do not fit neatly within traditional guidelines, not because they are unusual, but because lending needs are diverse. When a loan falls outside standard residential structures, it often follows a different risk-evaluation approach, including how credit is reviewed.

These loan categories are not exceptions created on the fly. They are established segments of the lending market with their own structures, goals, and evaluation models. Because they are built differently, they may not rely on the Middle Credit Score® in the same way standard residential mortgages do. That difference reflects the nature of the loan, not a judgment about the borrower.

Common examples of loan categories that fall outside standard residential guidelines include:

- **Non-QM loans**
- **DSCR loans**
- **Portfolio loans**
- **Certain investment-focused products**

What matters here is context. These loan types are designed around factors that differ from traditional owner-occupied residential lending. As a result, they may use different scoring approaches, consider alternative indicators, or follow internal guidelines established by the lender offering the product. None of this diminishes the role of the Middle Credit Score® in mainstream residential lending; it simply acknowledges that not every loan is built on the same foundation.

Understanding that these categories exist helps keep expectations aligned. It explains why someone may hear different terminology or encounter different standards depending on the type of loan being discussed. The distinction is structural, not personal, and recognizing that distinction is what allows the broader credit conversation to remain clear and grounded.

Why These Loans Use Different Evaluation Methods

Loans that fall outside standard residential guidelines are built to answer different questions. Because the loan structure is different, the way risk is evaluated must differ as well. This isn't a matter of being more or less strict; it is a matter of alignment. A loan designed for a non-traditional scenario requires an evaluation method that matches the nature of that scenario.

In these cases, lenders often view risk through a different lens. Instead of centering the decision on the same qualifying framework used for standard residential mortgages, they may weigh factors more relevant to the loan's purpose. That shift does not imply that credit is unimportant. It means credit is being considered in a broader or alternative context that better aligns with the loan's design.

Internal lender guidelines also play a larger role here. Because the same standardized residential frameworks do not govern these loans, lenders offering them may set their own evaluation criteria. Those parameters are meant to reflect how the loan performs, how it is repaid, and how risk is managed within that specific product, not to reclassify or judge the borrower.

The core point is simple: different loans require different lenses. When the structure of a loan changes, the evaluation method changes with it. That distinction is about loan architecture, not borrower quality. Understanding this helps keep the role of the Middle Credit Score® in proper perspective: central to standard residential lending but not expected to govern every lending scenario outside it.

Why This Does NOT Reduce the Importance of the Middle Credit Score®

It is easy to fall into the trap of thinking that if a rule has exceptions, the rule itself must be weak. In mortgage lending, the opposite is true. The importance of the Middle Credit Score® lies not in its use everywhere, but in where it is used. Standard residential mortgage lending sets the benchmark for how credit is evaluated across the industry, and that benchmark is built on consistency, scale, and repeatability.

Standard residential loans represent the core of the mortgage market. They account for the overwhelming majority of completed transactions and operate within nationally recognized frameworks. Within that environment, the Middle Credit Score® is not optional or situational; it is foundational. It exists because the system requires a reliable way to evaluate credit when multiple scores are present, and it has proven effective across millions of loans over many years.

Exceptions do not redefine that rule. Loans that fall outside standard guidelines are designed for specific use cases that require different structures and different evaluation models. Their existence does not weaken the standard; it confirms it. When a system is robust, it can accommodate specialized products without abandoning the framework that governs the majority of outcomes.

What ultimately matters is scope, not universality. The Middle Credit Score® matters because it applies where most borrowers live, borrow, and buy homes. Its role is central precisely because it governs the mainstream of residential mortgage lending. Understanding that distinction allows the framework to remain credible, grounded, and clearly defined without needing to stretch beyond the purpose it was designed to serve.

Takeaways

• The Middle Credit Score® is widely used, but not universal
• Some loan types intentionally operate outside standard residential guidelines
• These exceptions exist because loan structures differ, not because borrower quality differs
• The presence of exceptions does not weaken the Middle Credit Score® framework
• Understanding boundaries increases clarity, confidence, and trust in the system

This chapter explained where the Middle Credit Score® is applied in residential mortgage lending and identified the specific situations in which alternative credit evaluation methods are used. These exceptions are driven by loan structure and program design, not by borrower quality or inconsistency in lending standards.

The next chapter explains how mortgage lending interprets credit behavior over time once a qualifying score has been established.

Middle Credit Score® Fundamentals

"Key Definitions"

Exceptions (Boundaries)
Situations where the Middle Credit Score® is not the primary qualifying method because the loan follows different structures.

Standard Residential Guidelines
Mainstream mortgage underwriting frameworks used for the majority of residential loans.

Non-QM Loan
A non-qualified mortgage product that may follow alternative underwriting frameworks outside standard residential guidelines.

DSCR Loan
A debt service coverage ratio loan often used for investment properties, where evaluation may focus on property income rather than traditional borrower qualification.

Portfolio Loan
A loan kept by a lender rather than sold into standardized secondary market frameworks, often allowing internal underwriting criteria.

Middle Credit Score® Fundamentals

"Foundational Evaluation Principles"

1. A system is credible when its boundaries are clearly defined.

2. The Middle Credit Score® is widely used in standard residential lending, but it is **not universal**.

3. Exceptions exist because **loan structure changes**, not because the borrower is "worse."

4. Loans outside standard guidelines may use different evaluation methods because they answer different risk questions.

5. Exceptions strengthen the framework by keeping it accurate and honest.

Middle Credit Score® Fundamentals

"Calculation Scenarios"

Scenario A — Standard Residential Loan

Loan type: **Conventional**
Credit scores: **670 / 702 / 735**
☑ Middle Credit Score® = **702**
(Standard usage)

Scenario B — Loan Outside Standard Guidelines

Loan type: **DSCR investment loan**
☑ Borrower may hear different score language or evaluation approach
(Reason: the loan structure changes the evaluation method)

Scenario C — Portfolio Loan Context

Loan type: **Portfolio loan**
☑ Lender may apply internal guidelines, including alternative evaluation rules
(Reason: not governed by standard secondary market frameworks)

Middle Credit Score® Fundamentals

"Standardized Explanatory Language"

☑ **Approved Explanation**

"The Middle Credit Score® is the standard for most residential mortgages. Some loan types—like Non-QM, DSCR, and certain portfolio loans—operate under different guidelines, so they may use a different evaluation approach. That's about loan structure, not borrower quality."

☑ **Approved Explanation**

"Think of the Middle Credit Score® like the main rulebook for mainstream mortgages. Specialized loans use a different rulebook because the loan itself is designed differently—so the credit evaluation method may change too."

Middle Credit Score® Fundamentals

"Common Misconceptions"

Misconception #1: "If there are exceptions, the rule must not be reliable."
☑ Correction: Exceptions are a sign of a strong framework with clear boundaries.

Misconception #2: "If my loan doesn't use the middle score, something is wrong with me."
☑ Correction: It's structural because the loan is built differently.

Misconception #3: "Non-QM and DSCR loans are random or improvised."
☑ Correction: These are established loan categories with defined structures.

Misconception #4: "Exceptions reduce the importance of the Middle Credit Score®."
☑ Correction: The middle score remains central because it governs the mainstream majority.

Middle Credit Score® Fundamentals

SECTION III — WHY THIS MATTERS

Chapter 9:

One Score Can Change the Outcome

Quick Chapter knowledge verification framing

This chapter establishes the following conceptual understanding:

1. Explain why even a small score difference can change mortgage outcomes.

2. Understand how lending systems use **thresholds** to make consistent decisions at scale.

3. Explain the difference between human expectations ("close enough") and system structure (position matters).

4. Identify the three core outcome categories: **approval, conditional approval, denial.**

5. Describe why outcomes are structural, not personal.

Middle Credit Score® Fundamentals

One Score Can Change the Outcome

By now, you understand that credit is not evaluated casually in mortgage lending. You have seen how multiple scores exist, why variation is normal, and how the Middle Credit Score® brings structure to a system built on moving data. What often remains unclear, however, is how those numbers translate into real outcomes, approvals, conditions, or denials, and why a difference that feels small can still matter.

This is the point where many borrowers feel the most confusion. If credit reflects long-term behavior, responsibility, and consistency, it can feel unfair that a narrow difference in score carries weight. The emotional reaction is natural. From a human perspective, effort feels continuous, not segmented. From a system perspective, decisions must be consistent, even when situations feel close.

This chapter explains how outcomes are determined within a structured lending framework and why "almost" and "enough" function differently inside systems that operate at scale. Once that logic is clear, outcomes can be interpreted as the result of defined system thresholds.

What follows explains how one score can influence results, not to alarm you, but to remove the mystery. Understanding the structure behind outcomes is what allows you to experience the process without internalizing it.

Why One Score Can Matter

Many people instinctively believe that small differences in credit scores should not matter. If a score reflects long-term habits, responsibility, and effort, then a one-point or a few-point difference can feel meaningless, almost arbitrary. That belief is reasonable from a personal perspective. Credit feels human because effort is human. You pay bills, manage accounts, and make decisions over time. It makes sense to expect the system to view that effort with the same flexibility.

Lending systems, however, are not built to evaluate effort on a case-by-case basis. They are built to evaluate outcomes consistently across an enormous volume. When millions of decisions must be made using shared rules, the system has to rely on defined reference points. Those reference points are not judgments about worth or

89

responsibility. They are structural tools that enable decisions to be made consistently today, tomorrow, and across different lenders and markets.

This is where the disconnect often appears. Borrowers experience credit as a reflection of personal behavior over time. Lending systems experience credit as data that must be interpreted within a framework. Both perspectives are valid, but they operate at different levels. What feels like a small difference on an individual level can still carry weight within a system designed to apply rules uniformly.

Understanding this distinction matters before outcomes are ever discussed. Separating personal effort from system structure clarifies why a single score can influence outcomes within standardized frameworks. The number itself is not powerful because it defines you; it matters because it sits within a system that requires consistency to function at scale. That context explains how outcomes are produced within standardized lending frameworks.

How Thresholds Work (Conceptual, Not Technical)

Every lending system that operates at scale relies on thresholds, even when those thresholds are not visible to the borrower. This is not unique to mortgages or credit. Any system that must make large numbers of consistent decisions needs defined points where one outcome ends, and another begins. Without those reference points, decisions would become subjective, uneven, and unpredictable.

Thresholds exist to create clarity within the system by defining where one outcome ends and another begins. They allow lenders to evaluate applications using the same framework across time, markets, and borrowers. When everyone is measured against the same standards, outcomes can be compared fairly and applied consistently. This is how a national lending system avoids improvisation and bias, even when individual situations vary.

This is also where the idea of being "close enough" can feel frustrating. From a human perspective, proximity feels meaningful. If you are near a line, it can feel like you should be treated as if you crossed it. Systems, however, do not operate on proximity. They operate on position. A threshold does not interpret intent or effort; it simply marks where one category ends, and another begins, so decisions remain consistent.

Seen within this framework, the role of thresholds becomes easier to interpret. Thresholds are not moral judgments or personal evaluations. They are structural tools. Their purpose is not to reward or punish, but to create order in a process that must work the same way for everyone. Once that framework is clear, outcomes start to feel less arbitrary and more understandable, even when they are disappointing.

How Outcomes Change (Approval, Denial, Conditions)

Once thresholds are understood conceptually, it becomes easier to see how different outcomes emerge without attaching fear or meaning to them. Mortgage lending does not operate on a single yes-or-no decision. Instead, outcomes fall into a small number of structured categories that reflect how an application aligns with the system at that moment, not who the borrower is as a person.

At a high level, those outcomes typically look like this:

- Approval
- Conditional approval
- Denial

These categories exist to organize decisions, not to label borrowers. The same borrower, with the same long-term credit habits, can end up in different outcomes depending on timing, documentation, or how their credit aligns with the framework at that moment. Nothing about that shift means the borrower changed. It means the snapshot did.

A conditional outcome often surprises people the most. It can feel confusing because it sits between approval and denial, even though it is simply the system signaling that more clarity is needed. From the system's perspective, this is not hesitation or doubt; it is structure. Conditions exist to resolve uncertainty so the final decision can be made consistently rather than impulsively.

The key point here is that outcomes are structural, not personal. They result from where an application falls within an established framework at a specific moment in time. Understanding that distinction helps keep the conversation grounded. Instead of internalizing an outcome as a reflection of effort or worth, it can be seen for what it is: a position within a system designed to apply the same rules across millions of decisions.

Why "Close Enough" Still Isn't Qualifying

One of the most emotionally charged moments in lending comes from the idea of being "close." When a borrower is just on one side of a line, it can feel reasonable to expect flexibility. From a human perspective, effort feels continuous, not segmented. If you're nearly there, it is natural to believe that "almost" should count for something.

Systems, however, cannot operate on "almost" without breaking consistency. The moment a system treats proximity the same as position, the line itself loses meaning. If one application is treated as qualifying because it is close, then every application just beyond it becomes a new debate. Over time, that erodes fairness, predictability, and trust because decisions start to depend on interpretation rather than structure.

This is where the experience can feel unfair, even when it isn't personal. Borrowers are not reacting to the system itself, but to the mismatch between human expectations and the system's design. The system is not evaluating how hard someone tried or how reasonable their situation feels. It's applying a framework that must work the same way for everyone, every time, regardless of circumstance.

Understanding this doesn't make disappointment disappear, but it does change how it is interpreted. "Close enough" is not rejected because it lacks value. It is not qualifying because systems require firm lines to function at scale. Once that distinction is clear, the outcome feels less like a judgment and more like what it truly is: a position within a structure that applies uniformly, not selectively.

Takeaways

- Small score differences can matter because lending systems require consistency at scale
- Credit decisions are shaped by structure, not personal judgment
- Thresholds exist to create order, not to measure effort or intent
- Approval, conditional approval, and denial are outcomes, not labels
- Being "close" feels human, but systems must operate on firm lines
- Understanding the framework reduces shock and self-blame

This chapter explained how credit outcomes are determined within structured lending frameworks and why decisions are based on alignment with defined thresholds rather than personal judgment. Understanding this structure clarifies why outcomes can change from moment to moment and reduces confusion when results differ from expectations.

Up to this point, the focus has been on how credit is evaluated at specific points in time and why outcomes can differ depending on timing and thresholds. The next chapter shifts the lens from individual decisions to how mortgage lending evaluates credit behavior over time, emphasizing patterns and consistency rather than isolated snapshots.

Middle Credit Score® Fundamentals

"Key Definitions"

Threshold
A defined reference point where one lending outcome ends and another begins to ensure consistent decision-making.

Position vs. Proximity
Position means being above or below a threshold; proximity means being close. Lending systems operate on position, not proximity.

Structured Outcome
A result produced by an established lending framework (not a subjective judgment).

Conditional Approval
A structured outcome where the system requires additional clarification or documentation before final approval.

Snapshot
A point-in-time view of the borrower's credit/financial profile used to determine outcomes in that moment.

Middle Credit Score® Fundamentals

"Foundational Evaluation Principles"

1. Mortgage lending systems rely on thresholds to stay consistent at scale.

2. Small score differences can matter because thresholds create defined categories.

3. Outcomes are not labels, they are structured system results.

4. Conditional approval is not denial; it is the system reducing uncertainty before finalizing a decision.

5. "Close enough" cannot be treated the same as "qualifying" without breaking fairness and predictability.

Middle Credit Score® Fundamentals

"Calculation Scenarios"

Scenario A — One Point Matters

Threshold: **700**
Borrower score: **699**
☑ Outcome: **Does not meet threshold** (position matters, not proximity)
Borrower score: **700**
☑ Outcome: **Meets threshold**

Scenario B — Outcome Categories

Borrower meets threshold but missing documentation
☑ Outcome: **Conditional Approval**
Borrower meets threshold and documentation complete
☑ Outcome: **Approval**
Borrower below minimum required threshold
☑ Outcome: **Denial**

Scenario C — "Same borrower, different snapshot"

Borrower score today: **699**
Outcome: may fall below threshold
Borrower score 30 days later: **702**
☑ Outcome: **May fall above threshold**
Borrower did not change as a person — the snapshot changed.

Middle Credit Score® Fundamentals

"Standardized Explanatory Language"

✅ Approved Explanation

"In mortgage lending, decisions have to be consistent across millions of loans. That is why systems use thresholds. A one-point difference can matter—not because it defines you, but because it changes your position inside the framework."

✅ Approved Explanation

"Think of thresholds like a gate. Effort matters, but the gate still has a line. Lending does not judge how close you are—it applies rules consistently, so outcomes stay fair and predictable."

Middle Credit Score® Fundamentals

"Common Misconceptions"

Misconception #1: "A few points should not matter."
✅ Correction: In systems built on thresholds, small differences can change category placement.

Misconception #2: "A denial means I failed."
✅ Correction: Denial is a system outcome, not a personal label.

Misconception #3: "Conditional approval means the lender does not trust me."
✅ Correction: Conditions exist to resolve uncertainty, not to accuse the borrower.

Misconception #4: "If I am close enough, they should approve it."
✅ Correction: Systems operate on firm lines to preserve fairness and predictability.

Middle Credit Score® Fundamentals

Chapter 10:

How Rates, Approvals, and Pricing Really Work

Quick Chapter knowledge verification framing

This chapter establishes the following conceptual understanding:

1. Explain why mortgage pricing feels confusing even when the system is operating correctly.

2. Describe how **approvals, tiers, and pricing** work together inside structured lending frameworks.

3. Explain why **small score differences** can change pricing outcomes due to **tier classification**, not personal effort.

4. Understand how long-term cost is **duration-based and cumulative**, not fear-based or dramatic.

5. Explain why clarity beats guessing and how understanding pricing structure reduces borrower anxiety.

Middle Credit Score® Fundamentals

How Rates, Approvals, and Pricing Really Work

For many borrowers, pricing is where confusion peaks. Rates are discussed early, revisited later, adjusted, confirmed, and sometimes re-explained. Without context, it can feel like numbers change without warning or, worse, without reason. Even confident borrowers can feel unsettled when pricing does not behave as they expect.

That reaction is not a failure of understanding. It is the result of how mortgage pricing is presented versus how it works. Most people expect pricing to be singular and static: one clear number that reflects the full picture. Mortgage lending does not operate that way, not because it is opaque, but because pricing is tied to structure, categories, and long-term assumptions that aren't visible on the surface.

This chapter explains cause and effect: how credit outcomes connect to pricing, why small differences in pricing influence long-term costs, and how approvals, tiers, and pricing interact, how credit outcomes connect to pricing, why small differences can influence long-term cost. And why clarity matters more than guessing when numbers are involved.

Once you see how approvals, tiers, and pricing fit together, the process becomes more structurally interpretable. Not because the math disappears but because it finally makes sense.

Why Pricing Feels Confusing

Most people expect mortgage pricing to work the way prices do in everyday life: one clear number, explained upfront, that stays relatively stable once quoted. That expectation is not naïve, it is learned. From groceries to subscriptions to interest rates advertised in headlines, we're conditioned to believe there is a single, definitive price attached to a product. So, when mortgage pricing seems to shift, narrow, widen, or reappear differently at different moments, it can feel disorienting, even unsettling.

That sense of whiplash often comes from timing rather than inconsistency. Borrowers encounter pricing at different stages of the process, sometimes early, sometimes later, sometimes framed as an estimate, sometimes as a confirmation. Without understanding what stage they are in or what information they are relying on, changes can feel abrupt or contradictory. What is happening is that clarity is increasing over time, not that the price itself is behaving unpredictably.

Pricing also feels opaque because much of what influences it happens behind the scenes. Borrowers are rarely shown the structure that supports pricing decisions; they are shown the result. When inputs are invisible and outcomes are visible, the gap gets filled with assumptions. It's easy to interpret that gap as inconsistency, even when the system itself is operating in a very orderly way.

In this framework, the source of confusion is structural rather than procedural. Mortgage pricing is based on layered information that becomes more precise as the process progresses. Until those layers are understood, pricing can feel like a moving target. This chapter exists to make that structure visible, so the experience feels grounded rather than confusing, and predictable rather than arbitrary.

Credit Tiers (High-Level, No Numbers)

When people hear the word "tier," they often imagine a ranking system that labels borrowers as better or worse. That is not what tiers are designed to do. In lending, a tier is simply a way of grouping similar risk profiles so decisions can be made consistently. It is a structural tool, not a personal assessment. Instead of evaluating every borrower as a completely unique case, the system places similar profiles into the same category so outcomes can be applied evenly.

This grouping exists because large lending systems cannot price every loan from scratch. With millions of mortgages originated across different markets and time periods, consistency matters more than customization. Tiers create that consistency by allowing lenders to apply the same assumptions to similar situations. The purpose is to standardize interpretation across comparable profiles and make sure the same inputs lead to the same outcomes wherever the loan is originated.

Tier-based grouping reduces subjectivity within large lending systems. If every application were priced individually, outcomes would depend too heavily on interpretation, timing, or discretion. Grouping creates guardrails. It ensures that borrowers with similar credit characteristics are treated similarly, even when their applications are reviewed by different people, in different places, or at different times. That predictability is what allows the system to function at a national scale.

Most importantly, tiers are about organization, not judgment. They exist to translate complex credit data into a framework that the system can work with reliably. Understanding that helps reframe how pricing decisions are made. Instead of feeling arbitrary or personal, they begin to look like what they are: the result of a structured system that applies the same rules, the same way, to everyone.

Why Small Score Differences Can Change Pricing

Once you understand how tiers work, it becomes easier to see why small score differences can have outsized effects on pricing. Pricing doesn't react to effort, intent, or improvement in isolation; it reacts to category placement. When a credit profile moves from one tier to another, even by a narrow margin, it is treated as a different risk category within the system. The change is not interpreted as "slightly better" or "almost the same." It is interpreted as "now in a different group."

This is where classification effects can appear disproportionate. From a borrower's perspective, a small score change may reflect months or years of consistent behavior and careful management. From the system's perspective, that same change represents a shift in classification. Pricing structures are built around categories, not gradients. Once a profile moves to a different tier, the assumptions tied to that category change, and pricing adjusts accordingly.

That adjustment isn't a reaction to the individual borrower. It is a reaction to how the system manages risk at scale. Cost structures, reserves, and long-term performance expectations are organized around tiers, so outcomes remain predictable across millions of loans. When a profile lands in a different category, the pricing reflects the expectations of that category, not a judgment about how close the borrower was to another line.

Understanding this helps bridge the emotional gap between personal experience and system behavior. Small differences feel personal because effort feels personal. Pricing changes feel abrupt because categories are set in stone. But the logic behind them is consistent. The system isn't responding to how hard someone tried; it is responding to where the credit profile sits within a framework designed to apply evenly, not interpretively.

Long-Term Cost (Plain Math, No Fear)

When people hear that small pricing differences matter, it's easy to assume the impact must be dramatic or immediate. In reality, the effect is cumulative and duration-based, and much steadier. Mortgage lending is long-term by design. Because payments are spread out over many years, even modest differences don't announce themselves all at once. They show up gradually, through repetition, not shock.

This is simply how math behaves over time. A mortgage doesn't magnify change through urgency or pressure; it magnifies it through duration. Small differences are applied repeatedly across hundreds of payments. Each payment may feel nearly identical to the last, but the cumulative effect reflects the structure that was set at the beginning. This reflects the long-term application of a fixed pricing structure. It is arithmetic doing what arithmetic always does when time is involved.

In long-term lending, pricing reflects duration rather than urgency. It is about recognizing that long-term lending turns structure into outcome. Pricing is not designed to surprise borrowers; it is designed to remain stable over the life of the loan. Once terms are set, the math unfolds predictably, without emotion or intention. The system is not leaning on pressure; it's relying on consistency.

Seeing it this way reframes the conversation. Long-term costs are not a warning; they are an explanation. It clarifies why categories, tiers, and pricing structures matter, even when the differences between them seem small at the start. When you understand that the impact comes from time rather than intensity, the process feels less intimidating and far more transparent.

Why Clarity Beats Guessing

When pricing feels confusing, the most common response is guessing. People try to fill in gaps with assumptions, fragments of advice, or numbers they have heard in passing. That guessing creates stress because it turns uncertainty into self-questioning. Instead of understanding what's happening, borrowers are left reacting to impressions, changes, or conversations without a clear framework to anchor them.

Clarity changes that experience entirely. When you understand how pricing is structured and why it behaves the way it does, you no longer need to interpret every shift emotionally. The process stops feeling unpredictable. You may not like every outcome, but you can recognize it as the result of a defined system rather than a moving target. That understanding stabilizes interpretation of pricing information, even when the numbers themselves do not change.

This is where interpretation becomes more consistent. Not because anything was optimized, fixed, or adjusted, but because the rules are no longer hidden. When you know how outcomes are shaped, you stop bracing for surprises. You are no longer guessing what matters or why something changed. The system becomes intelligible, and intelligibility replaces anxiety.

That calm understanding is intentional. Before moving forward, it is important to see how credit, thresholds, tiers, and long-term cost all fit together without urgency or pressure. The next chapter builds on this clarity by shifting focus from pricing outcomes to how lenders interpret stability over time. This is where the conversation moves from structure to durability and where understanding becomes even more grounded.

Takeaways

- Mortgage pricing feels confusing because it becomes clearer over time, not because it is inconsistent.
- Lending systems use tiers to create consistency at a national scale, not to judge individual borrowers.
- Small credit score differences matter when they move a borrower from one category to another, not because effort changed, but because classification did.
- Pricing reacts to structure, not intent or proximity.
- Long-term costs are shaped by duration and repetition, not by sudden changes or pressure tactics.
- Understanding how pricing works reduces emotional volatility, even when outcomes aren't ideal.

This chapter explained how mortgage pricing operates within structured tiers and why small score differences can affect outcomes without reflecting changes in borrower behavior. It clarified how pricing responds to classification and duration rather than intent, proximity, or short-term movement.

The next chapter examines how mortgage lenders evaluate credit behavior over time, focusing on patterns, consistency, and durability rather than on individual moments or categories.

Middle Credit Score® Fundamentals

"Key Definitions"

1. **Mortgage Pricing**
   The system used to convert borrower classification and loan structure into rate, cost, and approval outcomes.

2. **Pricing Layers**
   The staged information inputs that become clearer over time (verified credit, documentation, structure), making pricing more precise.

3. **Credit Tier**
   A category used to group similar risk profiles so pricing and approval outcomes can be applied consistently at national scale.

4. **Classification Effect**
   The system outcome that occurs when a borrower moves into a different pricing category—causing changes that feel disproportionate to the score difference.

5. **Long-Term Cost (Duration Effect)**
   The cumulative cost impact that results when a small pricing difference repeats over hundreds of mortgage payments.

Middle Credit Score® Fundamentals

"Foundational Evaluation Principles"

1. Mortgage pricing feels like it changes because **clarity increases over time**, not because the system is inconsistent.

2. Pricing is based on **structure**, not emotion because borrowers see outcomes before they see inputs.

3. Tiers exist to create **consistency at scale**, not to judge borrowers as "better" or "worse."

4. Pricing changes most often when **category placement changes**, not when effort changes.

5. Long-term mortgage cost grows through **duration and repetition**, not urgency or pressure.

Middle Credit Score® Fundamentals

"Calculation Scenarios"

Scenario A — Tier Threshold (Classification Effect)

Tier line: **700**

- Borrower Score: **699** → Category A
- Borrower Score: **700** → Category B

☑ Result: Even a 1-point shift can change tier classification and pricing because **the system reacts to category placement.**

Scenario B — Duration Effect (Long-Term Cost)

Loan Term: **30 years (360 payments)**

Pricing difference: small change in rate/cost

☑ Result: The cost difference is not dramatic *today* — it becomes meaningful because it repeats **360 times**.

Scenario C — Pricing "Moves" But Becomes More Accurate

Stage 1: early estimate (limited verified inputs)

Stage 2: verified documents + confirmed credit + clarified structure

☑ Result: pricing doesn't "drift"; it instead becomes **more precise** as the layers become visible.

Middle Credit Score® Fundamentals

"Standardized Explanatory Language"

☑ **Approved Explanation**

"Mortgage pricing is not one fixed number early on, it becomes clearer as more verified information is added. That is why pricing may shift, not because the system is inconsistent, but because it's becoming more accurate."

☑ **Approved Explanation**

"Tiers are not personal rankings. They are categories that keep decisions consistent across millions of loans. Small score changes can affect pricing when they move you into a different tier—because pricing reacts to structure, not intent."

Middle Credit Score® Fundamentals

"Common Misconceptions"

Misconception #1: "If the rate changes, the lender is changing the rules."

☑ **Correction:** The rules did not change; the **inputs became clearer**. Pricing feels different because borrowers often see pricing outcomes before they see the layered structure behind them.

Misconception #2: "Tiers are a ranking system meant to label borrowers."

☑ **Correction:** Tiers are not judgment, they are **organization**. Without tiers, large lending systems would become subjective, inconsistent, and unpredictable across different lenders and markets.

Misconception #3: "If I improved my score a little, pricing should improve a little."

☑ **Correction:** Systems do not price using "gradual effort." They price using **categories**. If a small improvement doesn't move tier placement, pricing may not change, because classification did not change.

Misconception #4: "If pricing differences matter, it must be a pressure tactic."

☑ **Correction:** Long-term cost differences are not fear—they are **math**. Mortgages amplify small differences through **time**, not intensity. It is repetition, not manipulation.

Middle Credit Score® Fundamentals

Chapter 11:

What to Focus On (And What to Ignore)

Quick Chapter knowledge - Verification Framing

This chapter establishes the following conceptual understanding:

1. Explain why credit feels overwhelming due to **noise**, not because credit is broken.

2. Identify which credit signals mortgage lending responds to (**durable signals**) versus which signals are distractions.

3. Understand why **patterns over time** matter more than isolated score movement.

4. Explain why consumer credit tools can increase anxiety by highlighting movement without context.

5. Describe why the Middle Credit Score® acts as a **stabilizing reference point**, not a shortcut.

Middle Credit Score® Fundamentals

What to Focus On (And What to Ignore)

By this point in the book, you have been introduced to more credit-related concepts than most consumers ever see laid out in one place. Multiple scores. Thresholds. Tiers. Outcomes. Pricing structure. None of it is complicated on its own, but taken together, it can start to feel like too much. When everything feels important, it becomes hard to know what deserves your attention.

That overload is not accidental. Credit information is everywhere, presented constantly, and rarely prioritized. Scores update—alerts fire. Numbers fluctuate. Advice comes from every direction. The result is noise, lots of signals competing for your focus, even when nothing meaningful has changed. For many borrowers, the anxiety does not come from their credit itself. It comes from not knowing which signals matter and which ones do not.

This chapter exists to quiet that noise, not by adding new rules, strategies, or action steps but by narrowing the lens. When you understand what mortgage lending responds to, much of the background chatter loses its power. The goal here is not control. It is clarity. Once you know what matters and just as importantly, what does not, you can move through the process with far less tension and far more confidence.

Why Credit Feels Noisy

For most people, credit doesn't feel confusing because it's complicated; it feels confusing because there is simply too much of it. Scores, alerts, updates, notifications, summaries, and dashboards all compete for attention, each claiming to be important. Over time, that constant stream creates the impression that credit is something that must be watched closely, interpreted constantly, and reacted to immediately. Even when nothing is changing, it can feel like something always *might* be.

This noise is not accidental. Modern credit information is designed to be visible, engaging, and persistent. Tools meant to increase awareness often end up increasing vigilance instead. When you are exposed to frequent signals without context, your mind fills in the gaps. A number moves slightly. An alert appears. A message uses urgent language. None of these things means a problem exists, but together, they can create the sense that credit is fragile or unstable, even when it is not.

More information doesn't automatically lead to more clarity. In fact, without structure, it often does the opposite. When everything is highlighted, nothing stands out. Important signals get buried alongside minor fluctuations, and meaningful patterns are obscured by constant updates. The result is mental clutter: too many inputs, not enough understanding of which ones matter in a mortgage context.

This is how anxiety creeps in quietly. Not because credit is failing, but because attention is being pulled in too many directions at once. When credit feels noisy, the problem is rarely the data itself; it is the lack of perspective around it. This chapter begins by lowering the volume, so the rest of the conversation can focus on clarity instead of constant monitoring.

What Actually Moves Mortgage Outcomes

Despite the abundance of credit information, mortgage outcomes are influenced by a relatively small set of core signals. Lenders are not weighing every detail equally or reacting to every fluctuation. At scale, decision-making must stay focused. The system is designed to look for indicators that reliably predict performance over time, not to be distracted by every data point that happens to be available.

This is why consistency matters more than volume. A thick credit file filled with activity does not automatically carry more influence than a simpler one. What matters is whether the behavior shown is steady, repeatable, and aligned over time. Mortgage lending responds to stability far more than it responds to noise. A pattern that holds tells the system something meaningful. Isolated moments do not.

Patterns are how the system separates signal from distraction. A single late payment years ago, a brief balance change, or a short-term fluctuation alone does not define an outcome. What matters is how credit behaves over longer stretches, whether obligations are managed consistently, whether changes settle, and whether the overall picture aligns. Patterns provide context. Context creates confidence.

Understanding this shifts attention away from the urge to monitor everything and toward recognizing what the system reacts to. Mortgage outcomes are not moved by the intensity of observation or by reacting to every update. They move when core signals align in a way the framework recognizes as durable. Once that is clear, much of the surrounding noise begins to fade on its own.

What Sounds Important (But Usually Isn't)

A lot of credit information feels urgent simply because it is visible. Alerts, notifications, and changing numbers are designed to catch attention, not to explain relevance. When something flashes, updates, or moves, it creates a sense that action is required even when nothing meaningful has changed. The emotional weight comes from presentation, not importance.

Visibility is not the same as influence. Many signals that feel loud to consumers play little to no role in mortgage outcomes. They exist because modern credit tools surface everything they can measure, often without context. When all data is presented side by side, it is natural to assume all of it carries equal weight when actually, most of it does not.

Consumer-facing tools tend to amplify this effect. They are built for engagement and awareness, not for clarity in underwriting. By highlighting frequent updates and micro-changes, they unintentionally train people to react to movement rather than meaning. That reaction can create anxiety even when the underlying credit profile is stable and aligned.

Examples of common distractions include:

- Frequent score fluctuations are shown day to day
- Alerts tied to minor balance changes or inquiries
- Multiple scores are displayed without an explanation of the purpose
- Visual warnings or color changes that imply urgency

Understanding this helps separate signal from noise. The goal is not to dismiss information, but to recognize that not everything you can see is something the mortgage system is responding to. Once that distinction is clear, the emotional charge around these distractions begins to wane.

Why One Number Often Matters More Than Many

It can feel counterintuitive that a system built on so much data ultimately anchors decisions to a single reference point. After all, credit reports contain pages of history, multiple scores, and countless details. But lending systems do not function by weighing every input equally. They function by organizing complexity into something that can be applied consistently, fairly, and at scale.

This is where the Middle Credit Score® comes into focus, not as a shortcut, but as a distillation. Multiple inputs are reviewed, compared, and contextualized, but the final decision needs a stable anchor. The middle score serves that role because it reflects balance across sources without leaning on extremes. It allows the system to acknowledge variation without being driven by it.

What's important to understand is that this simplification does not erase nuance. Interpreting the full credit picture occurs before the anchor is set. By the time a qualifying score is referenced, the complexity has already been accounted for. The single number doesn't replace the data; it represents the point at which that data converges into an outcome the system can reliably act on.

In that sense, one number matters more not because it tells the whole story, but because it marks the conclusion of the review. It's where many signals converge into a single decision framework. Far from distorting reality, this approach makes decision-making clearer, more predictable, and less subjective for borrowers and lenders alike.

Takeaways

- Credit feels overwhelming, not because it's broken, but because too much information is presented without context.
- Mortgage outcomes are influenced by a small number of durable signals, not by constant monitoring.
- Patterns over time matter more than isolated changes or visible alerts.

- Many consumer-facing credit signals create urgency without influencing lending decisions.
- The Middle Credit Score® serves as a stabilizing reference point, not a shortcut.
- Clarity reduces anxiety more effectively than vigilance.

This chapter explained how mortgage lending filters large amounts of credit information by focusing on a small number of durable signals rather than constant changes or alerts. It clarified why monitoring every fluctuation does not improve outcomes and how the Middle Credit Score® functions as a stabilizing reference within that structure.

The next chapter examines how timing influences credit evaluation, explaining when credit information meaningfully affects mortgage decisions and when it does not.

Middle Credit Score® Fundamentals

"Key Definitions"

1. **Credit Noise**
   The constant stream of alerts, fluctuations, dashboards, and score movement that competes for attention without clear mortgage relevance.

2. **Signal vs. Noise**
   Signal = mortgage-relevant indicators that influence outcomes. Noise = visible changes that feel urgent but usually don't affect underwriting.

3. **Durable Signal**
   A credit indicator that reflects stable behavior over time and can predict long-term performance (patterns, consistency).

4. **Isolated Change**
   A one-off movement (minor score change, small balance update, a single alert) that looks important but often doesn't change mortgage outcomes.

5. **Stabilizing Reference Point**
   The Middle Credit Score® used as an anchor to organize and interpret multiple inputs without being driven by outliers.

Middle Credit Score® Fundamentals

"Foundational Evaluation Principles"

1. Mortgage outcomes are influenced by a **small set of core signals**, not by constant monitoring.

2. **Patterns over time** carry more weight than isolated changes or short-term movement.

3. Visibility is not influence: **what you see often matters less than what underwriting evaluates.**

4. Credit-monitoring tools surface "movement," but underwriting evaluates **meaning.**

5. The Middle Credit Score® is a stabilizer: it represents where multiple signals converge into a usable decision framework.

Middle Credit Score® Fundamentals

"Calculation Scenarios"

Scenario A — Noise That Feels Big (But Usually Isn't)

A consumer receives 3 alerts in 7 days:
- "Your score changed!"
- "Balance changed!"
- "New inquiry detected!"

Interpretation: These alerts create urgency, but unless they change qualifying score/tier, they are usually **noise**, not mortgage outcome drivers.

Scenario B — One Durable Signal That Matters

Credit report shows:
- Multiple accounts
- A consistent history of on-time payments over time

Interpretation: Underwriting values the **pattern** (durability), not the daily fluctuation.

Scenario C — Many Numbers, One Anchor

Scores: **682 / 701 / 739**

Middle Credit Score® = **701**

Why this matters: It filters complexity into a stable reference point so the system can make consistent decisions without reacting to extremes.

Middle Credit Score® Fundamentals

"Standardized Explanatory Language"

☑ **Approved Explanation**

"Credit monitoring tools create a lot of noise because they highlight movement. Mortgage lending doesn't react to every fluctuation, it focuses on durable patterns, consistency, and the qualifying score."

☑ **Approved Explanation**

"Not everything visible in credit matters to underwriting. Mortgage decisions are influenced by a few strong signals over time. The Middle Credit Score® acts as a stable anchor once the full credit picture has been reviewed."

Middle Credit Score® Fundamentals

"Common Misconceptions"

Misconception #1: "If I am getting alerts, something must be wrong."
☑ **Correction:** Alerts are designed for engagement. They signal *movement*, not mortgage relevance.

Misconception #2: "If my score changes weekly, my mortgage outcome will change weekly."
☑ **Correction:** Mortgage lending responds to durable signals and patterns, not every short-term shift.

Misconception #3: "More credit data means more certainty."
☑ **Correction:** More data without structure creates confusion. Underwriting reduces complexity by focusing on signals that predict stability.

Misconception #4: "If I just watch my credit closely enough, I can control the outcome."
☑ **Correction:** Outcomes change when the core framework signals change, not when anxiety-driven monitoring increases.

Middle Credit Score® Fundamentals

SECTION IV — EDUCATION BEFORE TRANSACTIONS

Chapter 12:

Why Education Comes Before Lending

Quick Chapter knowledge - Verification Framing

This chapter establishes the following conceptual understanding:

1. Explain why mortgage lending feels overwhelming when **outcomes arrive before understanding**.

2. Understand why **education before lending** reduces confusion, stress, and second-guessing.

3. Describe how informed borrowers interpret outcomes as **procedural, not personal**.

4. Explain how education improves the process for both borrower and lender by reducing friction and misinterpretation.

5. Understand why separating education from transaction reduces **pressure, bias, and urgency**.

Middle Credit Score® Fundamentals

Why Education Comes Before Lending

By the time most people encounter mortgage lending, they are already being asked to react. Numbers are presented. Decisions feel urgent. Outcomes arrive before understanding has had a chance to settle in. This sequence is so typical that it feels normal, but it is also the source of much of the confusion, stress, and second-guessing that surround the mortgage process. Confusion increases when lending interactions occur before structural understanding is established. It becomes confusing because it usually arrives before clarity.

This chapter examines the effects of reversing that order, placing understanding before action rather than after outcomes appear. When understanding comes first, everything that follows lands differently. Credit decisions are interpreted within context rather than as personal evaluation. Outcomes feel interpretable instead of shocking. Education does not eliminate responsibility; it strengthens it by giving meaning to the information borrowers are asked to respond to.

In mortgage lending, action taken without context often leads to misinterpretation. When people move forward without knowing how the system works, they tend to fill gaps with assumptions. Those assumptions create regret where none was necessary and anxiety where none was warranted. Education, placed before transaction, doesn't delay progress; it protects it. This chapter establishes that foundation, because everything that follows depends on it.

Why Informed Borrowers Make Better Decisions

Education does not make decisions hard; instead, it makes them steadier. When borrowers understand how mortgage lending works, they don't experience every update, number, or outcome as a surprise. Information stops feeling like something that happens *to* them and starts feeling like something they can place in context. That shift changes how data is processed and categorized. The facts do not change, but how they're interpreted does.

An informed borrower reacts differently to the same information because understanding creates orientation. When an outcome appears, it's not immediately internalized as a verdict or a setback. It's recognized as a result produced by a system with defined rules and structures. That recognition creates space between the event and the emotion. Instead of panic or self-blame, there's perspective. Instead of urgency, there's comprehension.

This does absolve responsibility; it does not guarantee favorable outcomes. Education does not insulate anyone from disappointment. What it does is prevent confusion from masquerading as failure. When borrowers know how decisions are made, they don't confuse *process* with *judgment*. They can acknowledge an outcome without attaching unnecessary meaning to it.

This orientation supports a more consistent interpretation of lending information, not because the borrower becomes more strategic, but because they become more centered. Decisions made from understanding tend to be measured instead of reactive. They are informed by clarity rather than pressure. Education doesn't push people forward faster or hold them back longer. It allows them to move through the process with awareness instead of apprehension, and that difference matters.

How Education Improves Outcomes for Everyone

When borrowers understand the structure they are moving through, the process encounters fewer interpretive interruptions; not because anyone is favored, but because fewer moments are misinterpreted. Education changes how information is interpreted, which reduces surprise during the process. Questions become more focused. Reactions become more measured. The process spends less time correcting misunderstandings and more time progressing with shared expectations.

Clarity changes the nature of interaction. Instead of reacting to individual moments in isolation, informed borrowers see how each step fits into a larger sequence. That perspective reduces friction. It limits second-guessing, emotional reversals, and unnecessary escalation. When people understand *why* something is happening, they're less likely to assume something has gone wrong.

This benefit is not one-sided. A process built on shared understanding tends to move more smoothly because the same information is interpreted through the same framework. That alignment doesn't eliminate complexity; it makes complexity manageable. Fewer explanations are needed because fewer misconceptions arise in the first place.

Education, in this sense, is not about empowering one side over another. It is about creating a common language. When everyone involved understands the structure, outcomes feel less adversarial and more procedural. That shared clarity doesn't promise better results; it creates better conditions. And better conditions allow the system to function with less strain and greater consistency for everyone involved.

Why Rushing Into Lending Creates Confusion

The impulse to move quickly is understandable. When someone is motivated, time-sensitive, or simply eager for answers, it can feel natural to say, "Just run it," or "Just tell me what happens." The intention is not careless; it is practical. But when action comes before understanding, the result is often confusion, not clarity.

Rushing tends to skip interpretation. Outcomes arrive before the framework needed to make sense of them. Numbers appear without context. Decisions are delivered without the structure that explains *why* they look the way they do. Without that grounding, even routine outcomes can feel abrupt or alarming, not because they're negative, but because they're unexpected.

As a result, early results are more likely to be misinterpreted than they are. When a borrower has not yet been oriented to how lending systems evaluate information, the first response is emotional rather than interpretive. The system speaks in outcomes, but the borrower has not yet been given the language to understand what those outcomes represent.

In many cases, the confusion is not caused by the result itself; it is caused by the order in which things happened. Action came first. Explanation came later. When education leads the process, outcomes tend to land with far less friction. Not because they change, but because they arrive in the correct sequence.

Separating Education from Transaction

When education stands on its own, it functions without transactional pressure. The moment learning is tied directly to a transaction, pressure enters the conversation sometimes subtly, sometimes immediately. Even well-intended explanations can feel loaded when there's an outcome waiting on the other side. Separation removes that weight. It allows understanding to exist without expectation.

When education is independent, it becomes neutral. There is no urgency to decide, no incentive to frame information a certain way, and no need to rush past complexity. The goal is not to move someone toward an outcome; it is to help them see the system clearly. That clarity builds trust precisely because nothing is being asked in return.

This separation also reduces bias, both perceived and real. When learning is not paired with action, information doesn't have to persuade or reassure. It can simply explain. Borrowers are free to absorb context, ask better questions later, and recognize how outcomes fit into a larger structure without feeling guided toward a particular conclusion.

Clarity is strongest when it isn't competing with momentum. Education that stands alone gives understanding room to settle before decisions are introduced. By keeping learning and doing distinct, the process becomes steadier, calmer, and more transparent, setting the stage for decisions that feel informed rather than pressured.

Takeaways

- Mortgage lending often feels overwhelming because outcomes arrive before understanding.
- Education doesn't slow progress; it stabilizes how information is received and interpreted.
- Informed borrowers don't react less; they respond with context rather than confusion.
- When understanding comes first, outcomes feel procedural rather than personal.
- Separating education from transaction removes pressure, bias, and unnecessary urgency.
- Clarity before action reduces regret, second-guessing, and emotional whiplash later.

This chapter explained why education placed before action stabilizes how mortgage information is interpreted and reduces unnecessary pressure during the lending process. It clarified how understanding provides context for outcomes without influencing or delaying them.

The next chapter examines how this understanding changes the borrower experience, focusing on how knowledge reshapes interpretation, emotional responses, and perceptions throughout the mortgage process.

Middle Credit Score® Fundamentals

"Key Definitions"

1. **Education Before Lending**
   A learning-first framework where the borrower understands the structure of lending before reacting to numbers and outcomes.

2. **Sequence Reversal**
   Reordering the mortgage experience so understanding comes first and outcomes arrive with context (education → action).

3. **Interpretive Framework**
   The mental structure that allows a borrower to understand outcomes as system-driven rather than emotional or personal.

4. **Transactional Pressure**
   The urgency and emotional weight introduced when learning is tied directly to a loan decision or outcome.

5. **Procedural Interpretation**
   Viewing mortgage outcomes as results of a consistent system rather than judgments about a person's worth or effort.

Middle Credit Score® Fundamentals

"Foundational Evaluation Principles"

1. Outcomes without context create confusion, so education must come first to create clarity.

2. Education does not remove responsibility; it strengthens it by making information meaningful.

3. Borrowers misinterpret results most often when action precedes understanding.

4. Shared understanding reduces friction, emotional escalation, and unnecessary second-guessing.

5. Education is strongest when separated from transaction because it removes pressure and perceived bias.

Middle Credit Score® Fundamentals

"Calculation Scenarios"

Scenario A — Action Before Education (Common Problem)

Borrower says: "Just run it."
Credit/outcome appears first → borrower feels shocked/anxiety.
☑ Result: reaction without framework = confusion, self-blame, second-guessing.

Scenario B — Education Before Action (Correct Sequence)

Borrower learns:
- what tri-merge is
- why scores differ
- what thresholds do
- why the Middle Credit Score® is used

Then credit is pulled and results appear.
☑ Result: outcomes feel understandable and procedural.

Scenario C — Education Separated from Transaction

Borrower receives education without a live loan decision pending.
☑ Result: less pressure, clearer thinking, better questions later, less emotional whiplash.

Middle Credit Score® Fundamentals

"Standardized Explanatory Language"

☑ Approved Explanation

"Education should come before lending because outcomes are easier to interpret when you understand the structure first. Learning does not delay the process; it stabilizes how you receive the information."

✅ **Approved Explanation**

"When borrowers understand the system before seeing the numbers, results feel procedural instead of personal. Education reduces confusion, pressure, and second guessing; even if the outcome doesn't change."

Middle Credit Score® Fundamentals

"Common Misconceptions"

Misconception #1: "Education slows down the mortgage process."
✅ **Correction:** Education does not delay progress, it reduces friction, misinterpretation, and emotional reversals that slow the process later.

Misconception #2: "If I just move fast, I will get clarity faster."
✅ **Correction:** Rushing often creates confusion because results arrive before you have the framework to interpret them.

Misconception #3: "Outcomes tell me what I am worth as a borrower."
✅ **Correction:** Outcomes reflect system position within a structured framework, not personal value or effort.

Misconception #4: "Explanations are biased because lenders want a certain outcome."
✅ **Correction:** Education is most trusted when separated from transaction because it removes pressure and makes learning neutral.

Middle Credit Score® Fundamentals

Chapter 13:

Why Certified Professionals Exist

Quick Chapter knowledge - Verification Framing
This chapter establishes the following conceptual understanding:

1. Explain why confusion in mortgage lending is usually caused by **inconsistent explanations**, not lack of information.

2. Define what "certified" means in principle: **alignment**, not status.

3. Understand why **alignment matters more than expertise** when education is involved.

4. Explain the difference between **education standards** and **professional opinions**.

5. Describe how consistency across professionals protects borrowers from **interpretive whiplash** and mistrust.

Middle Credit Score® Fundamentals

Why Certified Professionals Exist

By now, one theme should be clear: confusion in mortgage lending rarely comes from lack of information. It comes from inconsistency different explanations, different interpretations, and different conclusions drawn from the same underlying system. When borrowers hear one thing from one professional and something else from another, trust erodes not because anyone is dishonest, but because the system appears unstable.

This chapter addresses that instability at its source, not by elevating certain professionals above others, and not by introducing credentials as status markers, but by examining why alignment matters when education is involved. If education is meant to reduce confusion, it must be delivered consistently. And consistency does not happen by accident. It requires shared understanding.

In this context, certification is not about proving expertise; it exists to ensure that education is delivered through a shared language, grounded in the same foundational understanding. It exists to ensure that when professionals explain how credit, lending, and outcomes work, they are speaking from the same foundational framework, even if their experience, role, or perspective differs. Without that alignment, education fragments into opinion, and opinion reintroduces uncertainty.

This chapter explores why certified professionals exist at all, not as gatekeepers, not as authorities, and not as marketers; however, as a structural response to a simple problem: when education varies, understanding breaks down. Alignment is what allows education to do its job.

What "Certified" Means in Principle

At its core, "certified" does not mean accomplished, advanced, or superior. In principle, certification exists to signal alignment, not achievement. It indicates that a person is working from a shared framework, using the same definitions, assumptions, and educational foundations as others within the system. The purpose is not to elevate individuals, but to stabilize understanding across interactions.

This distinction matters because knowledge alone does not guarantee clarity. Two professionals can be equally informed and still explain the same concept in different ways. When that happens, borrowers aren't benefiting from expertise; they are navigating interpretation. Certification, in principle, exists to reduce that interpretive drift by anchoring explanations to common standards rather than personal phrasing or preference.

Seen this way, certification is not about what someone knows in isolation. It is about how that knowledge is expressed and applied in context. Collective consistency matters because education is not delivered once; it is reinforced across conversations, decisions, and moments of uncertainty. When explanations align, understanding accumulates. When they do not, confusion compounds.

The value of certification, conceptually, is that it prioritizes coherence over individuality. It does not diminish experience or insight; it channels them through a shared structure, so education remains steady regardless of who delivers it. In that sense, certification is less about validating professionals and more about protecting the integrity of the educational experience itself.

Why Alignment Matters More Than Expertise

Expertise, on its own, is not the problem. In fact, most confusion in mortgage lending does not come from a lack of knowledge, but comes from too much of it, expressed in too many different ways. Highly experienced professionals can explain the same concept accurately and still leave borrowers with very different impressions. The issue isn't competence. It is a variation.

From a borrower's perspective, inconsistency is indistinguishable from contradiction. When one explanation emphasizes caution, another emphasizes opportunity, and a third frames the same outcome as routine, the borrower is not hearing nuance; they are hearing conflict. Even when every explanation is technically correct, the lack of alignment makes the system feel unstable. Trust begins to wobble, not because anyone is wrong, but because nothing sounds settled.

This is how misalignment quietly shows up. A borrower hears one thing early, something slightly different later, and a third version when decisions become real. Each explanation may be rooted in experience, but together they create friction. The borrower is left trying to reconcile perspectives instead of understanding the process. What was meant to clarify ends up complicating.

Alignment matters because education is cumulative. Each conversation builds on the last. When explanations line up, understanding deepens. When they don't, borrowers are forced to reorient repeatedly, which creates fatigue and doubt. Over time, that doubt erodes confidence not just in the information, but also in the system that delivers it.

This isn't a critique of expertise. It is a recognition of its limits when operating without a shared structure. Expertise explains; alignment stabilizes. And in a process where borrowers rely on multiple professionals at different moments, stability matters more than any single explanation, no matter how well-informed it may be.

Education Standards vs. Opinions

Opinions are not a flaw in professional environments; they are inevitable. Experience shapes perspective, and perspective shapes how information is framed. Two professionals can look at the same situation, the same data, and the same outcome, and emphasize different aspects based on what they have seen before. That variation is human, and it is not something to eliminate. The challenge arises when opinions become the primary source of education rather than a layer applied after a shared foundation is established.

Education standards exist to provide that foundation. They do not replace professional judgment, nor do they demand uniform thinking. What they do is establish a common language, a shared baseline that ensures core concepts are explained the same way, in the same order, with the same underlying meaning. When that baseline is in place, opinions become additive instead of confusing. They build on understanding rather than reshaping it.

Without standards, interpretation fills the gap. Subtle differences in wording, emphasis, or framing can change how information is received, even when the facts are unchanged. Over time, those small shifts compound. Borrowers aren't just hearing different perspectives; they are receiving different versions of reality. Standards reduce that distortion by anchoring explanations to agreed-upon principles before interpretation enters the conversation.

This does not strip away nuance. In fact, it protects it. When the foundation is consistent, nuance can be introduced intentionally rather than accidentally. Borrowers can recognize the difference between what is structurally true and what is situationally interpreted. Education standards do not silence opinions; they give them a stable place to stand so understanding remains intact, even as perspectives vary.

Why Consistency Across Professionals Protects Borrowers

Consistency across professionals isn't about controlling conversations or limiting judgment; it is about protecting the borrower's experience. When explanations change depending on who someone speaks to, uncertainty fills the gaps. Even accurate information can feel unstable if it is framed differently from one interaction to the next. Consistency lowers that emotional volatility by ensuring that core concepts don't shift beneath the borrower's feet.

Aligned explanations reduce shock by creating familiarity. When borrowers hear the same foundational reasoning repeated across professionals, outcomes feel less abrupt and less personal. The system is starting to look coherent rather than fragmented. Even when the news is not what someone hoped for, it lands with context rather than confusion. That consistency matters in a process where decisions rely on structured interpretation.

Predictability doesn't mean promises. It doesn't guarantee outcomes or remove uncertainty from the process itself. What it does is allow borrowers to anticipate how information will be framed and why certain conclusions follow from certain inputs. When the logic is consistent, borrowers spend less time questioning whether something changed and more time understanding what's being communicated.

In that sense, consistency is a form of protection. It shields borrowers from interpretive whiplash, the stress that comes from hearing different explanations for the same reality. By aligning how education is delivered, professionals create an environment where understanding can take hold before emotion does. That environment does not eliminate risk or decision-making, but it does make the experience steadier, clearer, and far less disorienting.

Takeaways

- Confusion in mortgage lending is most often caused by **inconsistent explanations**, not a lack of information.
- Certification exists to create **alignment**, not hierarchy or status.
- Expertise without shared standards can unintentionally increase borrower confusion.
- Education standards provide a **common language** that allows nuance without distortion.
- Consistency across professionals protects borrowers from interpretive whiplash and misplaced mistrust.
- Certification, properly understood, is about **trust in the framework**, not trust in individuals.

This chapter explained why professional certification exists to preserve educational consistency, not to create hierarchy or advantage. It clarified how aligned standards reduce confusion by ensuring that explanations remain grounded in the same framework regardless of who delivers them.

The next chapter examines what happens when that alignment is absent, focusing on how inconsistent explanations and fragmented standards affect borrowers' understanding and experience throughout the mortgage process.

Middle Credit Score® Fundamentals

"Key Definitions"

1. **Certification (Alignment-Based)**
   A credential that signals the professional teaches from a shared framework using consistent definitions, assumptions, and order of explanation.

2. **Alignment**
   The practice of delivering explanations using the same foundational logic and language so education remains consistent across interactions.

3. **Interpretive Drift**
   The gradual distortion that occurs when professionals explain the same system in different wording, emphasis, or framing—creating confusion.

4. **Education Standards**
   Shared baseline definitions and sequence of explanation that ensure concepts are communicated consistently before nuance or opinion is added.

5. **Interpretive Whiplash**
   Borrower stress and mistrust caused by hearing conflicting explanations from different professionals about the same reality.

Middle Credit Score® Fundamentals

"Foundational Evaluation Principles"

1. Confusion most often comes from **variation in explanation**, not from missing information.

2. Certification should signal **coherence and consistency**, not hierarchy.

3. Expertise alone can increase confusion if there is no shared structure behind explanations.

4. Education standards must come before opinions, so nuance becomes **additive**, not destabilizing.

5. Consistency protects the borrower experience by making explanations predictable and outcomes interpretable.

Middle Credit Score® Fundamentals

"Calculation Scenarios"

Scenario A — Same Outcome, 3 Different Explanations

Borrower is told by 3 professionals:
- "You're not ready."
- "You're fine, just proceed."
- "This is risky—wait."

☑ Result: borrower hears contradiction → trust erodes even if all 3 are well-intentioned.

Scenario B — Alignment Creates Stability

Borrower speaks to 3 certified professionals:
All 3 explain the Middle Credit Score® the same way:
- same definitions
- same sequence
- same meaning

☑ Result: understanding accumulates; borrower confidence increases.

Scenario C — Standards + Opinion in the Correct Order

Professional explains:
1. structural foundation (standards)
2. THEN situational nuance ("in your case...")

☑ Result: borrower can separate **what is true structurally** from what is **interpreted situationally**.

Middle Credit Score® Fundamentals

"Standardized Explanatory Language"

✅ Approved Explanation

"Certification exists to ensure consistent education. It does not mean someone is 'better'—it means they are aligned with a shared framework, so borrowers receive stable explanations across different professionals."

✅ Approved Explanation

"Borrowers do not lose trust because people lie—they lose trust because explanations vary. Certified professionals protect the education experience by using shared definitions and standards before adding personal nuance."

Middle Credit Score® Fundamentals

"Common Misconceptions"

Misconception #1: "Certification means superior expertise."

✅ **Correction:** Certification is about **alignment**, not superiority. It signals shared educational structure, not status.

Misconception #2: "If professionals disagree, the system must be unstable."

✅ **Correction:** The system is often stable, while the explanations are not. Misalignment sounds like contradiction.

Misconception #3: "Opinions should replace standards because every case is unique."

✅ **Correction:** Standards come first so borrowers have a baseline. Opinions belong after, as nuance—not as the foundation.

Misconception #4: "Consistency limits professional judgment."

☑ **Correction:** Consistency protects borrowers. It does not eliminate judgment; it **anchors** judgment, so it does not distort understanding.

Middle Credit Score® Fundamentals

———————

Chapter 14:

Why All Advice Is Not Equal

Quick Chapter knowledge - Verification Framing
This chapter establishes the following conceptual understanding:

1. Explain why advice often sounds convincing even when it is misaligned with mortgage decisions.

2. Understand the difference between **general financial advice** and **mortgage-specific guidance**.

3. Explain why good intent does not guarantee accuracy in standardized lending frameworks.

4. Understand how confidence, familiarity, and repetition can make advice feel "true" without being verified.

5. Describe how standardized education creates a framework to interpret advice calmly and correctly.

Middle Credit Score® Fundamentals

Why Not All Advice Is Equal

Most advice is given with good intentions. People share what worked for them, what they have heard repeated, or what sounds reasonable based on their own experience. In everyday situations, that kind of guidance can be helpful. It builds connection, offers reassurance, and creates a sense that problems are solvable. The challenge isn't that advice exists; it is that not all advice is built for the same decisions.

In mortgage lending, context matters more than intention. The rules, structures, and evaluation methods that shape outcomes are specific, standardized, and often invisible to consumers. Advice that feels sound in a general financial sense can become misleading when applied to a mortgage decision, not because it is wrong in principle, but because it was not designed for that framework.

This chapter is not about telling you who to trust or who to ignore. It is not about attacking advice-givers, apps, platforms, or professionals. Most misinformation doesn't spread because someone is trying to deceive; it spreads because simplified guidance travels faster than nuanced explanation. Confidence gets mistaken for accuracy. Familiarity gets mistaken for relevance.

This chapter examines discernment rather than distrust. By understanding why advice can be well-meaning yet misaligned, you can place information in context rather than react emotionally. That skill does not make you skeptical; it makes you grounded. And in a process as consequential as mortgage lending, contextual accuracy matters more than frequency of opinion.

Why Does All Advice Sound Convincing

Advice tends to sound convincing because it is almost always delivered with certainty. People share guidance because they believe in it, because it worked for them, or because they have heard it often enough to feel settled. Confidence is commonly interpreted as reliability. When someone speaks clearly and decisively, it creates the impression that the information is reliable, even when the full context is not yet visible.

Familiarity deepens that trust. Advice from friends, family, coworkers, or commonly used tools feels approachable and low risk. It sounds like what we have heard before, or what we already expect to be true. That familiarity reduces friction. It does not feel like a claim that needs to be evaluated; it feels like shared knowledge passed along with good intent.

Repetition reinforces belief. When the same guidance shows up across conversations, articles, apps, or alerts, it begins to feel accurate simply because it's common. Frequency can quietly replace verification. Over time, repeated messages take on the weight of consensus, even when they have not been examined within a specific mortgage context.

Advice also spreads faster than explanation. Advice is concise, portable, and easy to repeat. Explanation requires sequencing, nuance, and patience. In environments where speed and clarity are valued, the shorter message usually wins. That does not make advice careless or misleading; by intent, it explains why it feels trustworthy so quickly. Recognizing this dynamic explains why advice often appears reliable before its relevance to a specific lending framework is evaluated.

General Advice vs. Mortgage-Specific Guidance

General credit advice exists to serve a wide audience. Its role is to promote awareness, encourage healthy habits, and help people stay engaged with their financial picture over time. In that sense, it does its job well. It offers broad principles that apply in many situations, without requiring deep context or specialized understanding. General advice is not designed to be precise; it is designed to be accessible.

Mortgage lending, however, operates within a far more specific framework. Decisions are made using defined structures, standardized evaluation methods, and long-term risk considerations that don't apply in every financial scenario. Because the context is narrower and the stakes are higher, the guidance that applies must also be more precise. What works as a general principle doesn't always translate cleanly into a mortgage decision, even when the intent behind the advice is sound.

This is where a mismatch can occur without anyone being wrong. Advice can be accurate in a general sense and still be misleading when applied to a mortgage context. The issue isn't quality or intent; it is scope. When guidance designed for broad use is applied to a specialized process, it can lose relevance without losing credibility. That subtle shift is often hard to detect, especially when the advice sounds familiar and reasonable.

In mortgage lending, information is interpreted within defined standards rather than loosely. It relies on defined standards and consistent evaluation. In high-stakes decisions, small contextual differences can change meaning. Understanding the difference between general awareness and mortgage-specific guidance does not require rejecting one in favor of the other; it requires recognizing which lens applies in which situation. That distinction is what keeps well-intended advice from being misapplied when precision matters most.

Why Intent Doesn't Guarantee Accuracy

Most advice is offered with genuinely good intentions. People share what helped them, what they have seen work before, or what feels logically sound based on their own experience. In many areas of life, that kind of shared insight is valuable. It builds connections, saves time, and helps others avoid obvious mistakes. The presence of good intent, however, does not ensure that the guidance fits every situation to which it is applied.

Experience is always contextual. What worked well in one financial decision, one market cycle, or one type of lending does not automatically translate to another. Mortgage lending operates within its own structures, timelines, and evaluation standards. When advice is carried over from a different context without adjustment, it can drift from accuracy even though the motivation behind it remains sincere.

In mortgage lending, accuracy is determined by framework rather than sincerity. A system interprets information according to defined rules, not personal logic. Advice that feels reasonable outside that framework may lose precision when applied within it. This is not because the advice is careless or irresponsible; it is because the lens through which it was formed does not align with the lens used to make the decision.

Confident misinformation often spreads unintentionally for this reason. When advice is delivered with clarity and conviction, it feels trustworthy. Confidence fills in for context, and repetition reinforces belief. Over time, guidance that is slightly misaligned can become widely accepted, not because anyone meant to mislead, but because the framework was never examined. Recognizing this distinction allows discernment without suspicion and understanding without blame.

Why Standardized Education Changes Everything

Standardized education does not exist to replace advice; it exists to give advice a frame. When information is anchored to a shared framework, it becomes easier to understand where guidance fits and where it doesn't. Context is what turns isolated statements into something usable. Without it, even accurate advice can feel confusing or contradictory. With it, information settles into place.

A shared educational framework reduces distortion by aligning how concepts are explained before interpretation enters the conversation. When core ideas are taught the same way, in the same order, with the same underlying logic, meaning does not shift from person to person. That consistency preserves definitional alignment across explanations. Differences in perspective can persist, but they rest on a stable foundation that maintains understanding.

This explains why consistency has a greater impact on understanding than the volume of advice available. Hearing the same concept explained clearly across different moments reinforces comprehension. Hearing many different explanations for the same idea fragments it. Standardized education does not add more voices; it aligns them, so understanding accumulates instead of resetting each time new information appears.

Standardized education functions as a reference framework rather than a decision filter. It doesn't ask you to ignore outside information or distrust what you hear elsewhere. It helps you recognize how that information fits or does not within the mortgage context. Education, when standardized, doesn't compete with advice. It gives you the structure to interpret it calmly, confidently, and without confusion.

Takeaways

- Advice can be sincere, confident, and widely repeated, yet still misaligned with mortgage decision-making.
- General financial guidance is designed for awareness, not precision; mortgage lending requires context-specific interpretation.
- Intent does not determine accuracy; the framework does.
- Discernment is not skepticism; it is the ability to place information where it belongs.

- Standardized education doesn't replace advice; it gives you a structure to interpret it without confusion.

This chapter explained why advice can be accurate in one context and misaligned in another, and why mortgage lending requires information to be interpreted within a specific framework. It clarified how discernment depends on context rather than intent, confidence, or repetition.

The next chapter examines how timing influences understanding, focusing on why the sequence in which information is introduced can shape whether mortgage decisions feel clear or confusing.

Middle Credit Score® Fundamentals

"Key Definitions"

1. **Discernment**

   The skill of placing advice into its proper context rather than reacting emotionally or assuming it applies universally.

2. **Mortgage-Specific Guidance**

   Guidance aligned with standardized mortgage lending rules, evaluation methods, and underwriting structures.

3. **General Financial Advice**

   Broad principles meant to promote awareness and good habits, not precision underwriting outcomes.

4. **Context Misalignment**

   When advice that is true or helpful in one setting becomes misleading when applied inside a mortgage framework.

5. **Standardized Education Framework**

   A consistent baseline structure that explains mortgage concepts using shared definitions and sequence before opinions are applied.

Middle Credit Score® Fundamentals

"Foundational Evaluation Principles"

1. Advice can be well-intended and still be wrong for mortgage decisions if it lacks proper context.

2. Confidence, familiarity, and repetition make advice sound reliable—even without verification.

3. General advice is meant for awareness; mortgage lending requires **precision within a defined framework**.

4. In lending, accuracy is determined by **framework**, not by sincerity or opinion.

5. Standardized education does not replace advice; it gives you a structure to interpret advice correctly.

Middle Credit Score® Fundamentals

"Calculation Scenarios"

Scenario A — Familiar Advice Misapplied

Friend says: "Just pay down any balance and your score will jump."

✅ Mortgage context reality: that advice may be generally helpful, but it may not change qualifying score/tier **within the mortgage decision timeline**.

Scenario B — Confidence Replacing Context

A person speaks decisively:
"This always works."

✅ Mortgage context reality: "Always" advice is risky because mortgage lending outcomes depend on standardized frameworks and timing.

Scenario C — Standardized Education = Interpretation Filter

Borrower learns standardized framework first:
- tri-merge
- middle score use
- thresholds/tiers

Then hears advice:
"You should wait 30 days before applying."

✅ Result: Borrower can interpret whether the advice fits the lending framework and timeline instead of reacting emotionally.

Middle Credit Score® Fundamentals

"Standardized Explanatory Language"

☑ Approved Explanation

"Advice can sound convincing because it is delivered confidently and repeated often. But mortgage lending requires context-specific guidance, and accuracy is determined by the framework, not by intention or familiarity."

☑ Approved Explanation

"General advice is designed to help many people stay aware of credit. Mortgage decisions are different. They run on standardized rules, so guidance must match the mortgage framework, not just sound reasonable."

Middle Credit Score® Fundamentals

"Common Misconceptions"

Misconception #1: "If advice is repeated a lot, it must be accurate."

☑ **Correction:** Repetition creates familiarity, not verification. Frequency can replace truth when context isn't examined.

Misconception #2: "If advice worked for someone else, it would work for me."

☑ **Correction:** Mortgage lending is framework driven. What worked in one situation may not apply in another loan type, market cycle, or timeline.

Misconception #3: "Good intent means good advice."

☑ **Correction:** Intent is emotional. Mortgage systems are structural. Accuracy depends on alignment with the lending framework, not sincerity.

Misconception #4: "Discernment means distrust."

☑ **Correction:** Discernment is not skepticism. It is stability, and the ability to place information where it belongs without confusion or emotion.

Middle Credit Score® Fundamentals

SECTION V — THE ECOSYSTEM (SOFT, NON-SALES)

Chapter 15:

Continuing Your Education at MiddleCreditScore.com

Quick Chapter knowledge - Verification Framing

This chapter establishes the following conceptual understanding:

1. Explain why mortgage and credit education is **ongoing**, not one-time.

2. Identify the difference between **self-guided learning** and **transaction-driven information**.

3. Explain what MiddleCreditScore.com exists to do; and equally important, what it does **not** do.

4. Understand why education works best as a **reference point**, not a directive.

5. Describe how pressure-free learning builds lasting clarity and confidence over time.

Middle Credit Score® Fundamentals

Continuing Your Education at MiddleCreditScore.com

By the time you reach this point, one thing should be clear: understanding credit and mortgage lending isn't something that happens all at once. It unfolds. Concepts connect. Perspective deepens. What began as clarification around scores, thresholds, and outcomes has gradually become something broader, a way of interpreting information without anxiety or distortion. That kind of understanding doesn't end when a chapter ends, and it doesn't need a transaction to continue.

Education, especially in an area as layered as credit and lending, works best when it is ongoing and self-directed. Questions don't always arrive on schedule. Sometimes they surface months later, triggered by a headline, a conversation, or a change in circumstance. When learning is framed as a one-time event, those moments can feel disruptive. When learning is continuous, it feels natural, simply the next point of reference.

MiddleCreditScore.com exists as a place where that continuity lives. Not as a replacement for this book, and not as a next step you're being guided toward, but as an extension of the same educational foundation. It is designed to hold explanations, context, and structure in one place, so understanding doesn't have to be rebuilt from fragments each time a new question arises.

This chapter is not about urging you forward or asking you to do anything. It is about orientation. If understanding matters, and by now, it should be clear why it does, then it helps to know where that understanding can continue to grow, at your pace, on your terms, without pressure. MiddleCreditScore.com is simply where the conversation stays available when you're ready to return to it.

Why Learning Is Ongoing, Not One-Time

Understanding mortgage lending rarely arrives all at once. Even when concepts are explained clearly, their meaning tends to deepen with exposure rather than settle immediately. What makes sense in theory often becomes clearer when it is encountered again, especially after time has passed or circumstances have changed. Learning, in this context, is not an event you complete. It's something that unfolds as understanding meets experience.

Different stages of life naturally surface different questions. What feels abstract early on can feel relevant later. What once seemed peripheral can suddenly matter. This is not a sign that something was missed the first time; it is how understanding works when information intersects with real situations. As context changes, familiar ideas take on new weight without needing to be relearned from scratch.

Many people return to education not because they failed to understand it before, but because experience has given them a new lens. A concept read years earlier may resonate differently after a conversation, a decision, or an outcome. Learning becomes less about acquiring new information and more about recognizing patterns that were always there, now seen more clearly.

This is why education around mortgage lending works best when it is treated as ongoing. Not continuous, not demanding, and not urgent, but available. Understanding is not something you lock in once and move past. It is something you revisit when the moment calls for it, bringing clarity forward rather than chasing it under pressure.

Self-Guided Education vs. Transaction-Driven Information

Self-guided education changes the way information is received. When learning happens without a decision waiting on the other side, the mind stays open instead of defensive. There is no pressure to act, no urgency to interpret everything correctly the first time, and no fear of getting something "wrong." Understanding has room to develop gradually, which is how complex systems are absorbed.

Transaction-driven information works differently. Even when explanations are accurate, they are often delivered at moments when outcomes matter immediately. That timing changes how information feels. Questions become loaded. Numbers feel heavier. Interpretation competes with emotion. The same explanation that would feel neutral in an educational setting can feel overwhelming when it's tied to approval, pricing, or next steps.

This is why timing matters as much as content. Learning is most effective when it arrives before pressure, not during it. When education comes first, information is processed as context rather than consequence. Concepts can be revisited, reflected on, and understood without the weight of an imminent decision shaping the response.

Self-guided education restores agency because it allows understanding to happen on your terms. You decide the pace. You decide what to revisit. Nothing is being framed to move you forward or hold you back. Education becomes what it's meant to be: orientation, not persuasion. That difference is subtle, but it is what makes learning stick.

What MiddleCreditScore.com Exists to Do (And Not Do)

MiddleCreditScore.com exists for one reason: education. Its purpose is to explain how credit is evaluated in mortgage lending, why certain outcomes occur, and how the system functions beneath the surface. It is designed to give context where most consumers are given conclusions. The focus is not on directing behavior, predicting outcomes, or steering decisions, but on making the structure visible so understanding can take root.

The site is intentionally narrow in scope. It centers on clarity, not optimization, explanation, not persuasion. Its role is to help readers understand concepts such as how credit scores are interpreted, why certain standards exist, and how lending frameworks operate at scale. It does not attempt to simplify the system through shortcuts, nor does it frame information to influence choices. The goal is comprehension, not momentum.

Equally important is what the site does *not* do. MiddleCreditScore.com is not a place to receive quotes, recommendations, or advice about what to do next. It does not sell products, promote transactions, or offer guidance tailored to individual situations. By maintaining this separation, the information remains neutral. Learning is allowed to stand on its own, without pressure or implied outcomes attached.

This boundary is what preserves trust. When education is not tied to selling or decision-making, it can remain honest, steady, and complete. Readers are free to engage with the material at their own pace, revisit concepts as needed and absorb understanding without urgency. MiddleCreditScore.com exists to support clarity, nothing more, and nothing less.

Education as a Reference Point, Not a Directive

Education is most useful when it supports decisions without trying to make them. Its role is not to point you in a specific direction or tell you what choice to make; it is to give you orientation. When understanding is solid, decisions don't feel forced or rushed. They feel informed, even when the outcome isn't obvious. Education becomes something you consult, not something that pushes.

This is the difference between instruction and reference. Instructions tell you what to do next. A reference helps you understand where you are. In mortgage lending, that distinction matters. When information is presented as a directive, it can create anxiety about choosing "correctly." When it is presented as context, it reduces that pressure. You are no longer worried about following steps; you are focused on understanding the landscape.

Reference-based learning works because it respects autonomy. It assumes that you can make decisions once the system makes sense. Instead of narrowing options or framing outcomes as right or wrong, education acts like a compass. It does not choose the path; it helps you recognize direction, boundaries, and terrain so your choices feel intentional rather than reactive.

Over time, this kind of learning builds quiet confidence. You do not need constant reinforcement or validation. When new information appears, you know how to place it. When outcomes arrive, you know how to interpret them. Education stops being something you lean on urgently and becomes something you carry steadily, available and free of pressure.

Takeaways

- Understanding credit and mortgage lending is **ongoing**, not event based.
- Education is most effective when it is **self-guided and pressure-free**.
- Learning works best when it arrives **before decisions**, not during them.
- MiddleCreditScore.com exists as an **education-first reference**, not a transaction or advice platform.
- Education functions best as a **reference point**, not a directive.
- Understanding retains value **even when no action follows**.

- Clarity does not demand urgency; it remains available when needed.

This chapter explained how education retains value independent of timing, decisions, or immediate action. It clarified why understanding functions best as a stable reference point rather than something that demands constant engagement or momentum.

The next chapter examines how understanding changes the borrower experience itself, focusing on how clarity alters interpretation, emotional response, and confidence throughout the mortgage process.

Middle Credit Score® Fundamentals

"Key Definitions"

1. **Ongoing Education**

   A learning process that deepens over time as experience intersects with understanding, rather than something completed once.

2. **Self-Guided Education**

   Learning that happens by choice, at your pace, without outcomes, pressure, or urgency shaping interpretation.

3. **Transaction-Driven Information**

   Information delivered in the middle of an active lending process, often under emotional pressure because an outcome is pending.

4. **Education-First Reference Platform**

   A resource designed to explain structure and context (not decisions), allowing readers to revisit concepts as needed.

5. **Reference-Based Learning**

   Education that offers orientation and interpretation tools rather than telling the reader what to do next.

Middle Credit Score® Fundamentals

"Foundational Evaluation Principles"

1. Education about lending works best when it is **available**, not urgent.

2. Learning deepens through repetition and real-life context—not because someone "missed it" before.

3. Transaction-based education feels heavier because outcomes are pending; self-guided education stays neutral.

4. MiddleCreditScore.com must remain **education-only** to preserve trust (no quotes, no selling, no individualized advice).

5. Education should function as orientation (context), not persuasion (directive).

Middle Credit Score® Fundamentals

"Calculation Scenarios"

Scenario A — Education During Pressure (Transaction-Driven)

Borrower is in active lending:
- rate changes
- conditions requested
- approval pending

☑ Result: even accurate information feels stressful because interpretation competes with emotion.

Scenario B — Education Without Pressure (Self-Guided)

Borrower learns:
- tri-merge
- score spread
- thresholds and tiers
  months before applying.

☑ Result: when outcomes arrive later, borrower interprets them calmly (framework already exists).

Scenario C — Reference vs Directive

Directive language: "Do this now."
Reference language: "Here is what this means."

☑ Result: education becomes a stabilizer, not a trigger for anxiety or rushed decisions.

Middle Credit Score® Fundamentals

"Standardized Explanatory Language"

☑ Approved Explanation

"Mortgage education works best when it is ongoing and pressure-free. You do not learn it once—you revisit it as life changes. That is why MiddleCreditScore.com exists as a stable reference, not a transaction platform."

☑ Approved Explanation

"MiddleCreditScore.com does not exist to tell you what to do next. It exists to explain what the system is doing and why, ensuring you can interpret outcomes with clarity instead of stress."

Middle Credit Score® Fundamentals

"Common Misconceptions"

Misconception #1: "If I have to revisit concepts, I did not understand them."

☑ **Correction:** Relearning is not failure; it is how understanding deepens when experience adds context.

Misconception #2: "The best education happens during the mortgage process."

☑ **Correction:** Learning under pressure is harder because outcomes create urgency. Education is strongest when it comes before the transaction.

Misconception #3: "Education platforms should give advice and next steps."

☑ **Correction:** Advice creates pressure and bias. A reference platform protects neutrality by explaining structure, not directing decisions.

Misconception #4: "If it does not push action, it is not useful."

☑ **Correction:** Education retains value even when no action follows—clarity stabilizes interpretation whenever the time comes.

Middle Credit Score® Fundamentals

Chapter 16:

When It Makes Sense to Speak With a Lender

Quick Chapter knowledge - Verification Framing

This chapter establishes the following conceptual understanding:

1. Explain why **timing matters more than urgency** in mortgage conversations.

2. Understand the difference between being **eligible** to speak with a lender and being **ready** to speak with one.

3. Describe why education should come **before** lender dialogue, not during it.

4. Identify what changes when readiness is present (interpretation becomes **structured**, not emotional).

5. Explain how alignment and shared language reduce friction and emotional volatility across conversations.

Middle Credit Score® Fundamentals

When It Makes Sense to Speak with a Lender

For much of this book, the focus has been intentionally upstream from action. You have been oriented to how credit is evaluated, why outcomes occur, and how structure, not judgment, shapes the mortgage process. That was deliberate. Mortgage conversations differ in effectiveness depending on whether a foundational understanding is present.

This chapter examines timing rather than urgency. There is a meaningful difference between being *eligible* to speak with a lender and being *ready* to do so. Eligibility is structural. Readiness is contextual. When those two align, the conversation tends to feel measured and productive. When they do not, even routine discussions can feel overwhelming or misinterpreted.

The question of *when* to speak with a lender often carries more emotional weight than it seems. Many people worry about engaging too early and feeling exposed, or too late and feeling behind. Those concerns are understandable, especially in a system where outcomes are often delivered without explanation. This chapter is not about setting a universal rule. It is about recognizing the conditions under which a conversation becomes useful rather than stressful.

The focus here is on noticing when readiness appears naturally, not as a push forward, and not as a signal that something must be done, but as an invitation to move from understanding into dialogue when it feels appropriate. When education has done its work, conversation shifts from exposure to structured dialogue. It starts feeling like the next step that makes sense.

Why Timing Matters More Than Urgency

In mortgage lending, timing is often confused with speed. People feel pressure to act quickly, to ask questions sooner, to "get ahead of it." That pressure usually isn't coming from the process itself; it comes from uncertainty. When understanding is incomplete, interpretation accelerates without structural reference. The conversation begins not because the moment is right, but because anxiety wants resolution.

Rushing a mortgage conversation does not usually create clarity. It creates noise. When questions are asked before the framework is understood, answers tend to feel heavier than they are. Numbers sound more final. Language feels more consequential. The same explanation can be interpreted differently depending on when it is introduced in the process, not because it changed, but because the listener was not ready to place it in context.

Urgency alters how information is processed. When someone feels pressed to act, information is filtered emotionally instead of structurally. Details are heard as signals. Possibilities are heard as outcomes. What is meant to orient ends up being internalized as pressure. This is why early conversations can feel more stressful than helpful, even when nothing negative is being said.

The same mortgage conversation can feel entirely different depending on when it happens. With understanding in place, the discussion feels exploratory and informative. Without it, the same words can feel exposing or definitive. Timing does not change the content; it changes how the content is received. That is why readiness matters more than speed and why waiting for the right moment is not hesitation, but alignment.

Education Before Conversation

Education changes the nature of a mortgage conversation before a single question is asked. When understanding is already in place, the discussion does not feel like a reveal; it feels like a continuation—information lands as confirmation rather than surprise. Instead of reacting to what is said, the listener recognizes the structure behind it, which immediately lowers emotional intensity.

Without that foundation, conversations tend to carry unnecessary weight. Answers feel decisive even when they are not. Language feels loaded because it is being interpreted without context. Education does not eliminate uncertainty, but it changes how information is contextualized. It allows the conversation to unfold as an explanation rather than an exposure, which is why the same discussion can feel calm in one moment and overwhelming in another.

Understanding also changes the kinds of questions that get asked. Not because someone is trying to ask "better" questions, but because clarity naturally narrows focus. When the framework is familiar, questions become more specific and less reactive.

They are aimed at understanding how things fit together, not at chasing reassurance or fast conclusions.

This explains why education typically precedes conversation rather than occurring during it. Learning first stabilizes interpretation before dialogue begins. When knowledge comes first, conversation becomes interpretive rather than emotional. The exchange feels grounded, not urgent. And that shift alone often determines whether the experience feels constructive or stressful, even when the information shared is the same.

What Changes When You Are Ready

Readiness does not change information content; it changes interpretive context. When context already exists, explanations no longer feel like a flood. They feel familiar, even when the details are new. The conversation moves at a steadier pace because understanding has somewhere to land. Nothing needs to be rushed past or emotionally buffered.

When readiness is present, explanations tend to settle rather than overwhelm. Language that once felt heavy becomes descriptive. Outcomes sound procedural rather than personal. This isn't because the stakes have changed; it is because the framework is already in place. You're not trying to orient yourself while processing new information at the same time.

Interpretive alignment replaces reactive interpretation. There is less second-guessing, not because answers are more favorable, but because they make sense within a system you recognize. You're no longer trying to decode meaning in real time. You understand why certain points matter, why others do not, and how the pieces connect without needing constant reassurance.

This distinction reflects the role readiness plays in interpretation. The conversation does not feel easier because it promises more; it feels steadier because it is grounded. Understanding does not change outcomes, but it changes how those outcomes are experienced. And in a process as consequential as mortgage lending, that distinction matters.

Why Alignment Improves the Experience

Alignment changes the texture of a conversation. When both sides are working from the same foundational language, less time is spent translating and more time is spent understanding. Questions do not need to be reframed repeatedly, and explanations do not feel like they are shifting underneath you. The exchange becomes clearer not because it is simpler, but because the same concepts are being referenced in the same way.

Shared language reduces the need for reinterpretation across conversations. When explanations align, you're not forced to reconcile competing interpretations or wonder which version is "right." Information builds instead of resetting. Each point connects to the last, creating continuity rather than fragmentation. That continuity is what allows conversations to feel steady instead of reactive.

Aligned explanations also prevent whiplash. In many mortgage conversations, the stress does not come from the information itself, but it comes from hearing it framed differently at different moments. Consistency removes that emotional jolt. When the reasoning stays the same from one discussion to the next, outcomes feel less abrupt and far less personal, even when they're significant.

Conversations do not happen in isolation, which is why consistency matters. They unfold over time, across questions, updates, and decisions. When alignment is present, each interaction reinforces understanding rather than challenging it. The experience remains coherent and predictable without altering outcomes.

Takeaways

- Speaking with a lender is most useful when it follows understanding, not urgency.
- Readiness is internal and contextual, not triggered by external timelines or pressure.
- The same mortgage conversation can feel clarifying or overwhelming depending on when it happens.
- Education before conversation changes interpretation, not outcomes.

- Alignment and shared language reduce friction and emotional volatility.
- A lender conversation is a transition into dialogue, not a commitment or irreversible step.

This chapter explained how timing and readiness shape the value of mortgage conversations, independent of urgency or external pressure. It clarified why education before dialogue improves interpretation and reduces friction without changing outcomes.

The next chapter examines how mortgage conversations are often misunderstood from the outset, focusing on communication gaps that arise even when information is accurate and intentions are aligned.

Middle Credit Score® Fundamentals

"Key Definitions"

1. **Eligibility**
   The structural ability to speak with a lender (having permission or capacity to begin the conversation).

2. **Readiness**
   The internal, contextual state where education and understanding are strong enough to interpret information without anxiety.

3. **Timing (Mortgage Context)**
   The point when a conversation becomes useful and measured because a framework for interpretation is already in place.

4. **Urgency**
   Emotion-driven pressure to act quickly, often triggered by uncertainty rather than by the actual process.

5. **Alignment (Shared Language)**
   When borrower and professional communicate using consistent definitions and frameworks, reducing reinterpretation and stress.

Middle Credit Score® Fundamentals

"Foundational Evaluation Principles"

1. Speaking with a lender is most productive when it follows **understanding**, not anxiety.

2. Readiness is not a deadline; it is an internal alignment between knowledge and timing.

3. Urgency distorts interpretation: possibilities get heard as outcomes, and explanations feel heavier than intended.

4. Education before conversation changes **interpretation**, not the lender's decision.

5. Alignment and consistent language reduce whiplash and increase conversation clarity across time.

Middle Credit Score® Fundamentals

"Calculation Scenarios"

Scenario A — Urgency Creates Noise

Borrower thinks: "I need answers now."
They call a lender early without framework.
☑ Result: language feels loaded, numbers feel final, anxiety increases.

Scenario B — Education Creates Productive Dialogue

Borrower learns first:
- tri-merge and score spread
- middle score logic
- thresholds and tiers
- outcomes vs judgment

☑ Result: conversation feels exploratory and confirming—not exposing.

Scenario C — Alignment Stabilizes the Journey

Borrower speaks with multiple professionals over time.
Without alignment:
- explanations vary → borrower feels system is unstable

With alignment:
- explanations build → borrower gains confidence and continuity

☑ Result: less second-guessing and emotional volatility.

Middle Credit Score® Fundamentals

"Standardized Explanatory Language"

☑ Approved Explanation

"It is not just about being eligible to speak with a lender, it is about being ready. Readiness means you have enough understanding to interpret the conversation structurally, not emotionally."

☑ Approved Explanation

"A lender conversation shouldn't feel like exposure or a test. When education comes first, the conversation becomes a calm dialogue which is informational, not urgent, and not irreversible."

Middle Credit Score® Fundamentals

"Common Misconceptions"

Misconception #1: "Speaking with a lender is a commitment."
☑ **Correction:** It is a transition into dialogue, not a binding step or irreversible move.

Misconception #2: "I should talk to a lender as soon as possible."
☑ **Correction:** Speed does not create clarity. Timing does. Urgency creates noise.

Misconception #3: "If I wait, I'm falling behind."
☑ **Correction:** Readiness is contextual, not based on external timelines. Alignment prevents misinterpretation.

Misconception #4: "If the conversation feels stressful, something must be wrong."
☑ **Correction:** Stress often comes from lack of framework, not from negative information.

Middle Credit Score® Fundamentals

SECTION VI — TRUST, IP, AND THE BIGGER PICTURE

Chapter 17:

Why Middle Credit Score® Is a Trademark

Quick Chapter knowledge - Verification Framing
This chapter establishes the following conceptual understanding:

1. Explain why widely used terms often experience **meaning drift** over time.

2. Understand why Middle Credit Score® is protected as a trademark to preserve **definition consistency**.

3. Identify how misinformation often spreads through **simplification**, not bad intent.

4. Explain how stable language allows education to **accumulate** instead of resetting.

5. Describe how consistent terminology builds **trust** through predictability in complex systems.

Middle Credit Score® Fundamentals

Why Middle Credit Score® Is a Trademark

By the time a concept becomes widely discussed, its meaning is already at risk of changing. Words get repeated, summarized, shortened, and adapted to fit different conversations. Over time, a term that once carried a precise definition can begin to feel familiar without remaining accurate. This is how misunderstanding spreads, not through bad intent, but through subtle drift.

When education is involved, language matters more than most people realize. A single phrase can shape expectations, emotional reactions, and decisions long before details are explained. If that phrase begins to mean different things to different people, definition consistency degrades. What was meant to orient starts to confuse. What was meant to explain starts to distort.

This chapter explains why the term Middle Credit Score® is protected not to claim ownership for its own sake, and not to restrict discussion, but to preserve meaning. When a term is central to understanding how a system works, consistency becomes essential. Without it, education fragments into interpretation, and interpretation reintroduces uncertainty.

Protecting terminology is about continuity. It ensures that when a concept is taught, referenced, or revisited, it still points to the same underlying structure. In the context of mortgage education, that stability allows understanding to build over time rather than resetting with each explanation. This chapter explores why that protection exists and why it matters for anyone seeking clarity rather than noise.

Why Terminology Protection Matters

Language does more than describe ideas; it shapes how they are understood. When a term is introduced to explain a complex system, its words carry structure, boundaries, and intent. Early on, that meaning is usually clear because it is closely tied to explanation. But as a phrase enters a broader conversation, it travels faster than its definition. The words remain, while the framework that gave them clarity slowly fades.

This is how commonly used terms evolve. They get repeated in summaries, shortened in conversation, and adapted to fit different contexts. None of this happens maliciously. It is a natural result of sharing ideas. But over time, repetition without precision changes meaning. What once pointed to a specific concept is now starting to feel flexible. Familiar, but less exact. The term sounds right, even when it's being used differently than intended.

When definitions blur, education weakens. Not because the idea itself is flawed, but because the language no longer anchors it. Two people can use the same phrase and mean different things, without realizing it. That disconnect creates confusion that's hard to trace, because the disagreement isn't obvious. Everyone believes they're talking about the same thing until outcomes don't line up with expectations.

This is especially important in mortgage education, where understanding depends on consistency. Systems rely on defined rules, not impressions. When terminology drifts, explanations start to vary. One version emphasizes one aspect, another emphasizes something else, and soon the original structure is obscured. The learner isn't missing information; they are receiving mixed signals built on the same words.

Terminology protection exists to prevent that drift. It is not about control or restriction. It is about preserving meaning, so education remains intact as it spreads. When a term keeps its definition, understanding can accumulate rather than reset. The goal isn't to limit conversation; it is to ensure that when a phrase is used, it still points to the same idea it was created to explain.

Preventing Misinformation Through Clarity

Misinformation rarely starts with bad intent. More often, it begins with simplification. An explanation gets shortened to make it easier to repeat, a concept gets summarized to fit a conversation, or a definition gets softened to sound more accessible. Each step feels harmless on its own. But as these simplified versions travel, they begin to replace the original meaning rather than point back to it.

Repetition accelerates this shift. When an idea is shared often enough, familiarity can stand in for accuracy. The words sound right, the phrasing feels settled, and confidence grows even if the explanation has slowly drifted from its source. Over time, the simplified version becomes the default reference, not because it's precise, but because it is easy to recall and easy to pass along.

Similar-sounding terms add another layer of confusion. When language is not clearly defined, people naturally assume equivalence where none was intended. A phrase designed to describe a specific framework starts to be grouped with broader, loosely related ideas. The distinction fades quietly. The learner is not misinformed because they ignored the explanation; they are misinformed because the explanation they received no longer matches the concept it was meant to represent.

Clear definitions limit this process before it compounds. When terminology is protected and consistently explained, reinterpretation has less room to take hold. Understanding does not depend on memory or assumptions; it remains anchored in meaning. That clarity doesn't eliminate conversation or variation, but it does ensure that the foundation remains intact as ideas move from one explanation to the next.

In practice, clarity produces the following effects:

- Simplified explanations remain connected to their original framework
- Similar terms are less likely to be treated as interchangeable
- Repetition reinforces understanding instead of reshaping it
- Confusion is reduced before it has a chance to spread

Clarity does not correct people after the fact; it prevents distortion from becoming normalized in the first place.

Consistency in Education Requires Stable Language

Education only works when people are learning the same thing. That may sound obvious, but it depends entirely on shared definitions. When language shifts, meaning shifts with it. Two people can use the same words and still be talking about different things if the definitions underlying those words are unstable. In education, that instability doesn't just slow learning, it fragments it.

Consistency allows understanding to accumulate. When a term means the same thing each time it is encountered, earlier explanations continue to support later ones. Concepts build on each other instead of needing to be reinterpreted. Learning becomes layered rather than repetitive. Without stable language, each explanation stands alone, and the learner is forced to reorient again and again, even when the topic hasn't changed.

Changing language resets learning because it breaks continuity. When terms are reused loosely or redefined informally, prior understanding no longer fits. What once felt clear becomes uncertain, not because the concept was flawed, but because the language around it shifted. This creates the illusion that the system is inconsistent, when it is the terminology that moved.

Protected terms function to prevent that reset. They act as anchors in the educational process, fixed reference points that allow meaning to remain intact over time. As explanations evolve, expand, or deepen, the underlying language stays steady. That stability is what makes long-term understanding possible, especially in subjects that are revisited across different stages, conversations, and experiences.

Stable language does not restrict learning; it protects it. By keeping definitions consistent, education becomes something that compounds rather than dissolves. Each interaction adds clarity rather than undoing it, and understanding can grow without quietly being reshaped along the way.

How stable language supports education:

- Shared definitions keep explanations aligned
- Consistency allows concepts to build instead of reset
- Learners recognize continuity across time and context
- Meaning remains intact as understanding deepens

How Stable Meaning Supports Trust

Trust in complex systems doesn't come from promises; it comes from predictability. When people hear the same term explained the same way across time and conversations, confidence builds quietly. Not because everything is certain, but because meaning feels stable. When definitions don't shift, borrowers stop wondering whether they misunderstood something earlier or whether the rules changed without notice.

Shifting language erodes confidence in subtle ways. A term that seems to mean one thing in one conversation and something slightly different in another creates friction. Even small differences in framing can trigger second-guessing: *Did I miss something? Did I misunderstand? Is this still the same thing?* That uncertainty is not about the decision itself; it is about whether the foundation beneath the explanation can be trusted.

Stable language reduces that mental load. When terminology remains consistent, borrowers do not have to re-evaluate what they are being told constantly. Explanations feel cumulative rather than corrective; instead of questioning whether information conflicts, people can focus on understanding how it applies. That steadiness lowers anxiety without requiring reassurance.

In systems as complex as mortgage lending, predictability matters. Not because it removes uncertainty, but because it creates orientation. When explanations stay aligned, predictability increases over time. Borrowers are not relying on authority; they are relying on consistency. And consistency, over time, is what allows trust to take root without being asked for or asserted.

Takeaways

- Language shapes understanding long before details are explained.
- When terminology drifts, education weakens even without bad intent.
- Protecting a term preserves meaning, not control.
- Stable language allows understanding to accumulate rather than reset.
- Consistency in wording builds trust quietly, through predictability.
- Clarity is sustained when concepts point to the same structure over time.

This chapter explained why protecting terminology preserves clarity, consistency, and cumulative understanding in mortgage education. It showed how stable language prevents conceptual drift and allows learning to build over time instead of resetting with each new explanation.

The next chapter examines how even clear terminology can break down in practice when communication lacks structure, and how misunderstandings can reappear during real-world conversations.

Middle Credit Score® Fundamentals

"Key Definitions"

1. **Terminology Drift**
   The gradual change of meaning that happens when a term is repeated, shortened, or adapted without its original definition.

2. **Definition Consistency**
   The requirement that a term mean the same thing across conversations, platforms, professionals, and time.

3. **Trademark Protection (Education Context)**
   Protecting a term to preserve its meaning and prevent misuse, so the concept remains tied to its intended structure.

4. **Conceptual Distortion**
   When simplified explanations evolve into a different concept than the original, even while using the same words.

5. **Cumulative Understanding**
   Learning that compounds over time because earlier explanations still match later explanations due to stable meaning.

Middle Credit Score® Fundamentals

"Foundational Evaluation Principles"

1. Language shapes understanding before details are ever explained definitions matter early.

2. When a term becomes popular, its meaning is at risk of drifting through repetition and simplification.

3. In education, unstable terminology causes learning to reset and creates confusion even when facts did not change.

4. Trademark protection is not about control, it is about protecting meaning, so education stays intact.

5. Consistent terminology builds trust through predictability and reduces second-guessing.

Middle Credit Score® Fundamentals

"Calculation Scenarios"

Scenario A — Definition Drift in the Wild

A person hears "Middle Credit Score" and assumes it means:

- an average score
- the highest score
- "my real score"

☑ Result: same words, different meanings → education breaks down.

Scenario B — Simplification Turns Into Misinformation

Original explanation:
"Mortgage lenders use the middle of the three bureau scores."
Simplified version spreads:
"They use *one* score and it is always the same."

☑ Result: simplification replaces the framework and becomes misinformation.

Scenario C — Stable Language Prevents Confusion

Protected term + consistent definition used across:

- book
- website
- certified professionals

☑ Result: each explanation reinforces previous understanding instead of contradicting it.

Middle Credit Score® Fundamentals

"Standardized Explanatory Language"

☑ **Approved Explanation**

"Middle Credit Score® is trademarked to preserve meaning. Without protection, terms drift over time, definitions blur, and education breaks down, even when no one intends harm."

☑ **Approved Explanation**

"The trademark is not about restricting conversation, it is about preventing confusion. When the definition stays stable, learning compounds, trust increases, and misinformation has less room to spread."

Middle Credit Score® Fundamentals

"Common Misconceptions"

Misconception #1: "Trademarking a term is about ego or control."
☑ **Correction:** In education-based systems, trademarking protects definition consistency and prevents distortion.

Misconception #2: "If people repeat the term, understanding increases automatically."
☑ **Correction:** Repetition without precision causes drift, while familiarity replaces accuracy.

Misconception #3: "Misinformation only spreads when people lie."
☑ **Correction:** Most misinformation spreads through simplification that slowly replaces the original framework.

Misconception #4: "Small definition differences don't matter."
☑ **Correction:** Small shifts compound over time and fracture education, causing trust erosion and confusion.

Middle Credit Score® Fundamentals

Chapter 18:

Protecting Clarity, Accuracy, and Consumers

Quick Chapter knowledge - Verification Framing
This chapter establishes the following conceptual understanding:

1. Explain how "protection" in mortgage education means **preventing confusion before it starts**.

2. Understand why standards exist to preserve meaning as education reaches **scale**.

3. Describe why accuracy matters more at scale (small misunderstandings **compound**).

4. Explain how education protects consumers by stabilizing **interpretation**, not limiting choices.

5. Understand how education protects over time by reducing confusion, regret, and emotional misreads later.

Middle Credit Score® Fundamentals

Protecting Clarity, Accuracy, and Consumers

When people hear the word "protection," they often assume oversight, enforcement, or restriction. In financial systems, protection is usually associated with rules designed to prevent harm after something has already gone wrong. But education operates differently. It protects long before decisions are made, outcomes occur, or conversations even begin.

In mortgage lending, confusion is rarely caused by missing information. It is caused by unclear language, inconsistent explanations, and ideas that lose precision as they spread. When understanding erodes, consumers are left vulnerable not because they were misled intentionally, but because the framework they needed was never stable to begin with. Protection, in this sense, is not about guarding against bad actors. It is about preserving clarity, so misunderstanding does not take root.

This chapter describes protection in educational rather than regulatory terms. It explores how accuracy, consistency, and clear definitions serve as safeguards not by limiting choice, but by strengthening interpretation. When consumers understand how a system works, they're less likely to misread outcomes, internalize confusion, or react emotionally to information that was never meant to be alarming.

Education functions protectively in a simple but powerful way: by preventing confusion before it starts, not through control, and not through restriction, but through clarity that holds steady over time. This chapter examines how that kind of protection works, and why it matters most when ideas reach scale.

Why Standards Exist at All

Standards do not appear because someone wants control; they emerge as systems scale and require stability. When ideas are shared within a small group, informal explanations work. Meaning can be clarified in real time, questions can be answered immediately, and misunderstandings are corrected naturally through conversation. But as education reaches more people, across more settings, that flexibility becomes a liability. What once worked through proximity begins to break down through repetition.

As systems grow, explanations travel farther than their original context. They are summarized, paraphrased, and adapted to fit new conversations. Each retelling introduces small variations not out of carelessness but out of convenience. Over time, those variations accumulate. The idea has not changed intentionally, but its edges soften. Meaning spreads faster than structure and understanding starts to fragment without anyone noticing.

Standards tend to emerge in response to that fragmentation. Their role is not to restrict explanation, but to preserve it. By anchoring key concepts to shared definitions, standards ensure that education remains recognizable no matter where it is encountered. They create continuity across interactions, allowing people to build understanding rather than recalibrate each time they hear the same idea explained slightly differently.

This distinction highlights the difference between standards and rules. Rules dictate behavior. Standards protect meaning. They do not tell people what to do; they clarify what something is. In education, that distinction matters. A standard doesn't narrow thought; it stabilizes it. It keeps learning intact as it moves through different voices, platforms, and experiences.

When education reaches the public, consistency is no longer optional. Without shared reference points, understanding dissolves into interpretation. Standards exist to prevent that not by asserting authority, but by ensuring that what's being taught today still means the same thing tomorrow.

Why Accuracy Matters at Scale

Accuracy matters at scale, not because perfection is required, but because small misunderstandings don't stay small once they're repeated. A single imprecise explanation might create mild confusion for one person. That confusion can be clarified, corrected, or simply fade away. But when the same explanation is shared widely, even slight distortions begin to multiply. What was once a nuance becomes a pattern. What was once a detail becomes an assumption.

Scale magnifies subtle shifts in meaning. When education reaches thousands or millions of people, minor inaccuracies are no longer isolated; they accumulate. Each retelling carries the version it received, not the version that was intended. Over time, these variations accumulate, quietly reshaping expectations. The original concept hasn't disappeared, but it's been blurred by repetition without precision.

This is why accuracy protects expectations, not outcomes. Education does not exist to guarantee results; it exists to help people understand how systems behave. When explanations are precise, expectations stay aligned with reality. People are less likely to feel surprised, misled, or confused by outcomes that follow. Accuracy does not change what happens; it changes how what happens is interpreted.

At scale, helpful education must be exact enough to travel intact. Not rigid, not technical, but clear. Precision keeps meaning from drifting as information moves through conversations, summaries, and interpretations. Without it, even well-intended education becomes harder to rely on, not because it's wrong, but because it no longer points consistently to the same thing.

Accuracy, then, is not about eliminating error; it is about preserving clarity as understanding spreads. It ensures that learning remains supportive rather than destabilizing, even as it reaches farther than any single explanation ever could.

Education as Consumer Protection

Education protects consumers not by restricting choices, but by shaping how information is received. When people understand how a system works, they are less likely to emotionally interpret every update, number, or outcome. Explanations land as context instead of verdicts. Education does not alter information; it establishes a consistent interpretive framework. And that shift alone can prevent confusion from turning into anxiety.

Informed consumers are less vulnerable to misunderstanding because they recognize structure. They know the difference between process and judgment, between movement and meaning. When something changes, it doesn't feel personal or alarming right away. Understanding creates orientation. Instead of reacting to fragments, people see how pieces fit together. That awareness reduces the likelihood that incomplete, or out-of-context information will be misread as a signal to worry.

Clarity also reduces pressure without limiting choice. When people know what information represents and what it does not, they do not feel pushed to act quickly just to regain a sense of control. Education reduces interpretive urgency created by unclear context. Choices remain open, but they're no longer made under the weight of confusion or imagined consequences.

In this way, education acts as a buffer, not a barrier. It does not stand between consumers and decisions; it stands between consumers and misinterpretation. Understanding stabilizes interpretation by maintaining consistent reference points as information is encountered. Protection, here, is not about guarding against action. It is about ensuring that when action eventually happens, it is grounded in clarity rather than confusion.

How Educational Protection Operates Over Time

The protection education provides doesn't begin and end with a single decision. Understanding carries forward, often quietly, shaping how future information is interpreted long after the original explanation is given. Once a framework is understood, it doesn't disappear when a conversation ends or a transaction pauses. It remains available, ready to be applied the next time questions surface or circumstances change.

This is why education continues to matter even when no action is taken. Understanding does not require momentum to stay relevant. It sits in the background, informing perspective without demanding attention. When new information appears months or years later, it is received within a familiar structure rather than as something entirely new. That continuity reduces the sense of being caught off guard and replaces it with a sense of recognition.

Clarity also reduces regret in subtle but lasting ways. Decisions made without understanding often feel heavier in hindsight, not because they were wrong, but because they were made without a stable frame of reference. Education provides that frame. Even when outcomes are uncertain or imperfect, understanding helps people make sense of what happened and why. That sense of coherence matters long after the moment has passed.

Protection, in this sense, persists beyond any single interaction. It does not depend on timing, outcomes, or follow-through. It shows up later, when information needs to be interpreted again, when memory alone would otherwise fill in the gaps. Education remains applicable across time, independent of transaction timing or outcome.

Takeaways

- Protection in mortgage education is not about restriction; it is about preventing confusion before it starts.
- Standards exist to preserve meaning as education reaches scale, not to control behavior.
- Accuracy matters because small distortions compound when repeated widely.
- Education protects consumers by stabilizing interpretation, not by limiting choice.
- The benefits of clarity persist long after conversations or decisions end.

This chapter explained how education functions as long-term consumer protection by preserving clarity, consistency, and meaning over time. It showed why understanding stabilizes interpretation without creating pressure, obligation, or urgency.

The next chapter shifts from systems and standards to experience. It examines how understanding interacts with emotion, expectation, and interpretation, and why clarity alone does not always prevent confusion.

Middle Credit Score® Fundamentals

"Key Definitions"

1. **Educational Protection**
   Protection created through clarity and understanding that reduces consumer vulnerability to confusion before decisions happen.

2. **Standards (Education Context)**
   Shared definitions and reference points designed to preserve meaning as ideas are repeated and spread.

3. **Accuracy at Scale**
   The need for precision because small distortions, when repeated widely, multiply into normalized misunderstanding.

4. **Interpretive Framework**
   A mental structure that helps people understand what information means (context), so they don't misread outcomes emotionally.

5. **Long-Term Protection**
   The continued benefit of education over time: future information is interpreted inside a familiar structure, reducing anxiety and regret.

Middle Credit Score® Fundamentals

"Foundational Evaluation Principles"

1. Protection in mortgage education is **not restriction**; it is preventing confusion early.

2. Standards preserve meaning when ideas travel beyond their original explanation.

3. In scaled education, small inaccuracies do not stay small, they **compound** through repetition.

4. Education protects by strengthening interpretation, not by controlling decisions.

5. Clarity persists and continues protecting consumers long after the conversation ends.

Middle Credit Score® Fundamentals

"Calculation Scenarios"

Scenario A — No Standards = Meaning Drift

A concept gets repeated across:
- social media
- conversations
- summaries

No shared definitions.

☑ Result: the meaning softens → confusion grows silently.

Scenario B — Small Inaccuracy at Scale

A slightly wrong explanation is repeated widely.

☑ Result:

1 person confused = easy fix

10,000 people confused = normalized misconception

Scenario C — Education as Consumer Protection

Consumer understands:
- what info represents
- what it doesn't
- how outcomes occur

☑ Result: less urgency, less emotional misinterpretation, more calm decision-making.

Middle Credit Score® Fundamentals

"Standardized Explanatory Language"

☑ Approved Explanation

"In mortgage education, protection does not mean restriction, it means preventing confusion before it starts. Clear definitions and consistent standards protect consumers by stabilizing how information is interpreted."

☑ Approved Explanation

"Education protects you long before a decision is made. It creates a framework so numbers and outcomes do not feel like judgments—they feel like information inside a system."

Middle Credit Score® Fundamentals

"Common Misconceptions"

Misconception #1: "Protection means enforcement or restriction."
☑ **Correction:** In education, protection means clarity that prevents confusion before harm happens.

Misconception #2: "Standards exist because someone wants control."
☑ **Correction:** Standards emerge because scaled education needs stability, and standards protect meaning.

Misconception #3: "Small inaccuracies do not matter."
☑ **Correction:** At scale, small distortions multiply into widespread misunderstanding.

Misconception #4: "Education is only useful right before a transaction."
☑ **Correction:** Education protects over time—months or years later—by preventing misinterpretation and regret.

Middle Credit Score® Fundamentals

Chapter 19
The Future of Credit Literacy in Homeownership

Quick Chapter knowledge - Verification Framing
This chapter establishes the following conceptual understanding:

1. Explain why credit literacy was historically **assumed**, not taught.

2. Understand why credit literacy matters more today due to **speed + visibility + constant signals**.

3. Identify how education changes a borrower's experience by stabilizing **interpretation**, even when outcomes don't change.

4. Understand the difference between being told information vs **owning meaning**.

5. Describe what the future of homeownership looks like when borrowers enter lending conversations with **structural clarity** instead of anxiety.

Middle Credit Score® Fundamentals

The Future of Credit Literacy in Homeownership

For most homeowners in modern times, credit literacy has been treated as something to be assumed rather than taught. Borrowers were expected to participate in complex systems without ever being fully oriented to how those systems worked. Explanations arrived late, if at all, and often only in response to outcomes that felt confusing or personal. The result was not ignorance; it was dependency. People learned to rely on interpretation instead of understanding.

This book approaches credit literacy differently. It has treated credit literacy not as background knowledge or optional context, but as something central to the experience of homeownership itself. Not because understanding guarantees better outcomes, but because it changes how outcomes are experienced. When borrowers understand structure, language, and intent, they stop interpreting every moment emotionally. They tend to recognize systems for what they are, rather than internalizing what they are not.

This final chapter looks forward not to predict where lending is headed, but to clarify what becomes possible when understanding is present. The future of credit literacy is not about new tools, platforms, or programs. It is about borrowers who are no longer dependent on fragments of advice or reactive explanations. It is about comprehension that stays intact over time, regardless of circumstance.

What changes when borrowers truly understand how credit and lending work is not the system itself; it is the relationship to it. Understanding can function as a form of ownership. Not ownership of outcomes, but ownership of meaning, and when meaning is owned, misinterpretation is reduced. This chapter closes the book by exploring that shift not as an aspiration, but as a foundation already within reach.

Why This Was Never Taught

For much of modern homeownership, mortgage credit literacy was not withheld; it was assumed. The system was developed with the expectation that borrowers would participate without needing a full explanation of how decisions were made. Credit reports existed. Scores were generated. Lending rules functioned in the background. The mechanics worked, so the need to explain them explicitly never became central.

Understanding was treated as implicit, something people would absorb along the way rather than something that needed to be taught upfront.

As lending systems evolved, they did so quickly and in a structural way. Automation increased. Standardization expanded. Decisions began to rely on models and frameworks that were efficient at scale but increasingly abstract to the people affected by them. The system learned how to move faster and more consistently, but consumer education did not evolve at the same pace. What changed behind the scenes was not matched by a corresponding effort to make those changes understandable to borrowers in plain terms.

Over time, assumptions filled the gap. It was assumed that basic explanations were sufficient, that familiarity would develop through repetition, and that outcomes themselves would teach what needed to be known. In practice, this meant many borrowers learned only after decisions were made, and often only the part that affected them directly. The broader structure remained invisible, not by design, but by default.

Over time, this contributed to a quiet distinction between information and understanding. Information was always available in documents, disclosures, numbers, and definitions. Understanding was not. Accessibility requires context, sequencing, and interpretation, not just data. When systems rely solely on availability, comprehension becomes uneven. Credit literacy didn't fail to exist; it simply wasn't built into the process as something that needed to stand on its own.

Why It Matters Now

What has changed is not the importance of credit, but the environment surrounding it. Mortgage lending has become faster, more visible, and more data-driven, while the underlying frameworks have grown more complex. Decisions are still made by structured systems, but borrowers now encounter them through dashboards, alerts, summaries, and fragments of information that were not part of the experience before. The result is greater exposure without greater understanding.

Modern borrowers are asked to interpret more signals than ever, often without a clear context for what those signals mean. Scores update. Numbers fluctuate. Language appears urgent. Information arrives continuously, but explanation does not. This creates a situation in which people are more informed than previous generations in volume, yet often less oriented toward meaning. The system has not become less fair or less functional, but it has become harder to intuit without guidance.

Speed compounds this gap. Information moves quickly, decisions feel closer together, and explanations are often delivered at moments when outcomes already matter. When understanding has not been established beforehand, even neutral information can feel consequential. Confusion carries a higher cost not because the stakes are new, but because interpretation happens under pressure. What once unfolded slowly now arrives all at once.

Visibility adds another layer. When systems were largely invisible, borrowers experienced outcomes without constant exposure to intermediate signals. Today, nearly every movement is surfaced. That visibility can be helpful, but without literacy, it can also magnify anxiety. Seeing more does not automatically mean understanding more. In many cases, it means reacting more.

This is why credit literacy matters now in a different way, not as an enhancement or advantage, but as a foundation. Understanding is no longer something that can be picked up passively over time. The environment demands orientation. Literacy has become the difference between feeling acted upon and feeling grounded, not because the system changed its intent, but because the way people encounter it has changed fundamentally.

How Education Shapes Empowerment

Empowerment in mortgage lending does not begin with action; it begins with interpretation. Before any decision is made, borrowers are already interpreting language, numbers, and outcomes. Without understanding, those interpretations are often emotional by default. Education shifts that posture. It does not give someone leverage or an advantage; it gives them a way to understand what they are seeing before reacting.

That change alters how information is interpreted throughout the process. Understanding changes how information lands. When borrowers recognize structure, explanations feel descriptive rather than decisive. Updates do not immediately register as signals of success or failure. Outcomes aren't internalized as judgments. This does not make the process easier in a practical sense; it makes it steadier. The emotional spikes flatten, not because outcomes improve, but because meaning is clearer.

This is why informed borrowers often experience fewer shocks, even when results are unchanged. The system behaves the same way it always has. What changes is the borrower's orientation to it. Education creates familiarity with process, language, and sequencing, so moments that once felt abrupt now feel expected. Not predictable in outcome, but recognizable in form.

In that sense, education can empower without promising anything. It does not optimize results or guarantee smoother paths. It stabilizes experience. Empowerment here is not about control or advantage; it is about steadiness. When understanding is present, borrowers are not bracing for the unknown.

That continuity reflects how education stabilizes interpretation across outcomes.

Understanding as Ownership

Ownership, in the context of credit literacy, is not about possession; it is about orientation. When someone understands how credit and lending work, they are no longer dependent on explanations to make sense of what's happening. Information doesn't have to be translated each time it appears. Meaning is already present. That shift from relying on explanation to holding understanding is what turns literacy into ownership.

This kind of ownership creates independence without isolation. Borrowers still engage with professionals, ask questions, and receive guidance, but they are no longer navigating mindlessly. They can listen, interpret, and contextualize what they are hearing without needing constant reassurance. Understanding does not replace conversation; it makes conversation functional instead of reactive.

Literacy also shifts power quietly, without confrontation. When understanding is in place, reactions soften. Instead of responding to information emotionally or defensively, borrowers respond with comprehension. They are not trying to keep up with explanations in real time; they recognize the structure beneath them. That recognition moves the experience from reaction to interpretation, which is where steadiness lives.

There is a meaningful difference between being told something and knowing what it means. Being told depends on timing, delivery, and trust in the source.

Knowing carries forward. It remains available when explanations end, and conversations pause. In mortgage lending, that difference matters because ownership of understanding changes how information is interpreted across contexts.

What the Future Looks Like

The future of homeownership does not hinge on faster tools, louder advice, or more information layered on top of what already exists. It looks quieter than that. It looks like borrowers entering conversations with a working understanding of the system they are stepping into, aware of how credit is interpreted, why outcomes occur, and what language means. Not because they memorized rules, but because the framework makes sense to them before anything is asked of them.

In that future, education is not a phase you move through and leave behind. It is a companion that stays available as circumstances change. Questions do not feel disruptive when they arise later, and new information does not feel destabilizing. Understanding travels with the borrower, ready to be applied when needed, without urgency or pressure. Learning becomes something that supports life decisions rather than interrupts them.

In practice, clarity tends to scale more effectively than control because it does not require enforcement to hold. When people understand how a system works, fewer explanations are needed to manage reactions. Expectations align more naturally. Interpretive inconsistency decreases as understanding increases, not because outcomes improve, but because interpretation does. A system grounded in clarity doesn't need to push or persuade; it simply makes sense, and that coherence does the work on its own.

This level of understanding provides a stable interpretive foundation for homeownership decisions. Not confidence rooted in certainty or outcomes, but consistency rooted in system comprehension. Borrowers know where they are, what information represents, and how to interpret what comes next. Decisions don't feel rushed, delayed, or reactive. They feel proportionate to the moment they are made.

That is what changes when credit literacy is treated as essential rather than optional. Understanding becomes something people own, not a tool they borrow or a process they endure. And when meaning stays intact, interpretive stability does not require reinforcement. It emerges naturally, supported by clarity that remains steady long after the final page.

Takeaways

- Credit literacy was never absent; it was simply assumed instead of taught.
- Understanding change experience, even when outcomes remain uncertain.
- Empowerment comes from interpretation, not leverage or action.
- Ownership of meaning replaces dependency on explanation.
- Clarity, not control, is what allows confidence to endure over time.

These are not instructions. They are conclusions the reader arrives at organically.

Middle Credit Score® Fundamentals

"Key Definitions"

1. **Credit Literacy (Homeownership Context)**
   The ability to understand how mortgage credit systems work, including language, structure, and outcomes so information is interpreted correctly.

2. **Interpretive Stability**
   The borrower's ability to process outcomes and updates calmly, because meaning is anchored in understanding rather than emotion.

3. **Empowerment (Mortgage Education Context)**
   Confidence created by interpretation and clarity—not by leverage, control, or guaranteed outcomes.

4. **Ownership of Meaning**
   The shift from depending on explanations to holding understanding; being able to interpret credit signals without panic or reliance on fragments.

5. **Clarity at Scale**
   A system-wide condition where consistent education reduces confusion across large populations without needing enforcement, pressure, or control.

Middle Credit Score® Fundamentals

"Foundational Evaluation Principles"

1. Credit literacy was not missing historically, it was **assumed**, and that assumption created dependency.

2. In the modern mortgage environment, more information creates more anxiety unless literacy exists.

3. Empowerment doesn't come from action; it comes from **interpretation**.

4. Understanding does not guarantee outcomes, but it **changes how outcomes are experienced**.

5. The future of mortgage education depends on **clarity and stable meaning**, not louder advice, more tools, or more alerts.

Middle Credit Score® Fundamentals

"Calculation Scenarios"

Scenario A — Assumed Literacy vs. Taught Literacy

A borrower receives:
- scores
- disclosures
- pricing
- outcomes

But no framework.

☑ Result: reliance on interpretation, stress, second-guessing.

Now compare:

Borrower receives:
- scores + system framework + meaning

☑ Result: the same information feels stable, not personal.

Scenario B — "More Information" Without Literacy

Borrower receives daily:
- score changes
- alerts
- warnings
- urgent language

☑ Result: "exposure increases" BUT "orientation decreases."

➡ **Visibility without literacy = anxiety multiplier.**

Scenario C — Ownership of Meaning Over Time

Borrower learns:
- what signals matter
- what signals do not
- why outcomes occur

Months later, a new situation appears.

☑ Result: borrower does not need "translation"—they already hold meaning.

➡ **Understanding becomes durable.**

Middle Credit Score® Fundamentals

"Standardized Explanatory Language"

☑ **Approved Explanation**

"Credit literacy is not about controlling outcomes. It is about understanding meaning, so updates, decisions, and numbers do not feel personal or confusing."

☑ **Approved Explanation**

"When you understand how mortgage credit works, you do not need constant reassurance. You can interpret information calmly, because you already know what it represents and why it happens."

Middle Credit Score® Fundamentals

"Common Misconceptions"

Misconception #1: "Credit literacy wasn't taught because borrowers didn't need it."

☑ **Correction:** It was not withheld, it was **assumed**, and the cost was dependency and confusion.

Misconception #2: "More credit tools and alerts mean consumers are more informed."

☑ **Correction:** They are more exposed, not more oriented. **More signals without literacy increases anxiety.**

Misconception #3: "Empowerment comes from negotiating power or special access."

☑ **Correction:** In mortgage lending, empowerment is mostly **interpretive**—knowing what information means before reacting.

Misconception #4: "Understanding is only useful when you're actively getting a mortgage."

☑ **Correction:** Understanding travels with the borrower over time. Literacy works as a **long-term foundation**, not a one-time tool.

Middle Credit Score® Fundamentals

Understanding how mortgage credit works does not require action, preparation, or next steps.

Once the framework is clear, it remains available whenever it is needed.

This publication exists to define structure, preserve meaning, and provide a stable reference for how the Middle Credit Score® functions within mortgage lending systems.

No decisions are implied.
No outcomes are promised.
No progression is required.

That is the purpose of fundamentals.

Glenn Clark is a real estate and mortgage professional with nearly three decades of experience working across every major function of the residential lending ecosystem. His career spans roles as a Loan Officer, Sales Manager, Director of Business Development, and Co-Owner of a mortgage company, as well as serving as a licensed Real Estate Broker and Owner of a real estate firm. This breadth of experience has given him a rare, end-to-end view of how mortgage credit is evaluated, explained, and ultimately experienced by consumers.

Glenn is a graduate of Arizona State University's W. P. Carey School of Business, where he earned a degree in Business Entrepreneurship. His professional background combines operational lending expertise with systems thinking—an approach that has shaped his work in mortgage education and platform design.

He is the founder of **Browse Lenders®** (BrowseLenders.com), a national platform built to connect consumers and professionals with vetted lenders who operate within standardized, transparent frameworks—including those aligned with Middle Credit Score® education. The platform was designed to reduce confusion, improve alignment, and create consistency in how mortgage credit is explained and applied.

The concept of **Middle Credit Score®** was created and trademarked by Glenn after decades of observing the same recurring problem across the industry: consumers, referral partners, and even professionals frequently misunderstood how mortgage credit scores are actually used. While millions of borrowers are approved each year using their middle credit score, the mechanics behind that process were rarely explained clearly or consistently. The result was confusion, misinterpretation, unnecessary cost, and missed opportunities.

Glenn recognized that the issue was not access to credit, tools, or data but the absence of a standardized educational framework. Middle Credit Score® was developed to preserve clarity, stabilize meaning, and ensure that professionals and consumers alike understand how mortgage credit functions within real-world lending systems.

His work also reflects a broader concern for the professionals who support homeownership decisions. Glenn has long advocated for realtors, real estate agents, HR teams, union benefit managers, CPAs, and financial planners to understand the role of the middle credit score—not to perform credit repair, but to properly orient clients and employees before lending decisions occur. In his experience, informed guidance upstream often prevents costly outcomes downstream.

Today, Glenn continues to focus on education, system alignment, and consumer protection through clarity. He is the author of *What Is Your Middle Credit Score?* and *Middle Credit Score® Fundamentals* and holds both a registered trademark and a pending patent related to the Middle Credit Score® educational framework.

He lives with his wife, their two children, and their dog, and remains actively involved in advancing credit literacy as a foundation for sustainable homeownership.

Appendix A — Definitions (Alphabetical Reference)

Accuracy at Scale
The requirement for precision in educational language because small distortions, when repeated widely, compound into normalized misunderstanding.

Alignment
The practice of delivering explanations using shared definitions, assumptions, and sequence so education remains consistent across interactions.

Alignment (Shared Language)
When borrowers and professionals communicate using the same definitions and frameworks, reducing reinterpretation and confusion.

Authorization
The borrower's written or documented permission allowing a lender to order and review a mortgage credit report.

Authorized Use
The approved use of the Middle Credit Score® name, definitions, and educational materials by certified professionals or affiliated organizations in alignment with official standards.

Baseline Standard
The default evaluation method applied in mainstream mortgage lending before exceptions or alternative structures are considered.

Calculation Scenario
A structured example used to illustrate how mortgage credit concepts function under defined conditions.

Certification (Alignment-Based)
A credential indicating the holder teaches mortgage credit concepts using standardized definitions, structure, and explanatory order.

Classification Effect
A system outcome that occurs when a borrower moves into a different pricing or eligibility category, resulting in changes that may appear disproportionate to the score movement.

Clarity at Scale
A system-wide condition where consistent education reduces confusion across large populations without enforcement, pressure, or control.

Conditional Approval
A structured lending outcome requiring additional documentation or clarification before final approval.

Conceptual Distortion
When simplified explanations evolve into a meaning different from the original concept while using the same terminology.

Consumer Credit Score (Monitoring Score)
A score viewed through consumer credit monitoring tools, designed for awareness and trends rather than mortgage underwriting.

Consumer Credit Tool
A platform built for general credit awareness and monitoring, not for underwriting or mortgage qualification decisions.

Context Misalignment
When advice that is valid in one setting becomes misleading when applied within a mortgage underwriting framework.

Credit Categorization
The classification of credit accounts (e.g., revolving, installment) that influences how scoring models interpret behavior.

Credit Inquiry (Mortgage Inquiry)
A visible record indicating a lender reviewed credit during the mortgage process; it reflects access, not a negative event by itself.

Credit Literacy (Homeownership Context)
The ability to understand how mortgage credit systems work, including language, structure, and outcomes, so information is interpreted correctly.

Credit Noise
The constant stream of alerts, fluctuations, and dashboards that create distraction without mortgage relevance.

Credit Reporting Organization (Credit Bureau)

A company that collects, organizes, and maintains consumer credit information reported by creditors.

Credit Tier

A category grouping similar borrower risk profiles so pricing and eligibility outcomes can be applied consistently at scale.

Cumulative Understanding

Learning that compounds over time because definitions and explanations remain consistent across contexts.

Debt Service Coverage Ratio (DSCR) Loan

An investment-focused loan evaluated primarily on property income rather than borrower income.

Definition Consistency

The requirement that a term retain the same meaning across conversations, platforms, professionals, and time.

Discernment

The ability to place advice into proper context rather than reacting emotionally or assuming universal application.

Durable Signal

A credit indicator reflecting stable behavior over time that is predictive of long-term performance.

Education Before Lending

A framework where understanding of structure precedes interpretation of outcomes.

Education Standards

Shared baseline definitions and explanatory sequence used to preserve meaning across education.

Education-First Reference Platform

A resource designed to explain structure and context rather than direct decisions.

Educational Protection

Protection created through clarity and understanding that reduces consumer vulnerability to confusion before decisions occur.

APPENDIX

Eligibility
The structural ability to begin a mortgage conversation based on permission or capacity.

Empowerment (Mortgage Education Context)
Confidence created through interpretation and clarity, not leverage, control, or guaranteed outcomes.

Equifax / Experian / TransUnion
The three primary credit reporting organizations used in the United States.

Exceptions (Boundaries)
Situations where the Middle Credit Score® is not the primary qualifying method due to alternative loan structures.

Fairness
A lending principle where no single unusually high or low score defines a borrower's entire profile.

General Financial Advice
Broad guidance intended for awareness and habits, not precise underwriting outcomes.

Independent Credit File
Each bureau's separate credit record; there is no shared or synchronized file.

Interpretive Drift
The gradual distortion that occurs when professionals explain the same system using different framing or emphasis.

Interpretive Framework
A mental structure allowing information to be understood as system-driven rather than personal.

Interpretive Stability
The ability to process outcomes calmly because meaning is anchored in understanding rather than emotion.

Interpretive Whiplash
Stress caused by receiving conflicting explanations about the same mortgage reality.

Isolated Change
A single data movement that appears significant but typically does not affect mortgage outcomes.

Knowledge Gap
Credit availability without credit context, leading consumers to misinterpret relevance.

Long-Term Cost (Duration Effect)
The cumulative impact of small pricing differences repeated over the life of a mortgage.

Long-Term Protection
The lasting benefit of education that supports future interpretation without urgency or regret.

Middle Credit Score®
The credit score between the highest and lowest of the three mortgage credit scores pulled at the same time for underwriting purposes.

Middle Credit Score® Identification
The standardized method of determining the middle score by comparing three scores and selecting the value between the highest and lowest.

Middle Credit Score® Language
The approved vocabulary and phrasing used to explain the concept consistently and accurately.

Middle Credit Score® Standard
The formal set of definitions, rules, and communication guidelines governing proper usage of the concept.

Middle Score
The score that falls between the highest and lowest bureau scores.

Mortgage Credit Evaluation
A structured underwriting review requiring consistency and context beyond consumer tools.

Mortgage Credit Pull
A lender-ordered credit review completed with borrower authorization.

Mortgage Credit Score (Underwriting Score)
A score used in mortgage underwriting decisions based on mortgage-specific scoring models.

Mortgage Pricing
The system translating borrower classification into rate and cost outcomes.

Mortgage-Specific Guidance
Guidance aligned with standardized mortgage underwriting frameworks.

Non-QM Loan
A non-qualified mortgage using alternative underwriting frameworks.

Ongoing Education
A continuing learning process where understanding deepens over time through repeated exposure, updated standards, and applied experience.

Outlier Score
An unusually high or low score caused by timing, reporting gaps, or bureau differences.

Ownership of Meaning
The shift from relying on explanations to holding understanding independently.

Patterns vs. Perfection
A lending principle prioritizing long-term behavior over flawless history.

Point of Balance
The concept that the middle score provides the most stable representation by avoiding extremes.

Portfolio Loan
A loan retained by the lender, often using internal underwriting criteria.

Position vs. Proximity
A lending interpretation principle: **position** means being above or below a defined threshold, while **proximity** means being close; lending outcomes are determined by position, not closeness.

Predictability
A repeatable evaluation method producing consistent outcomes across borrowers and time.

Pricing Layers
The staged underwriting inputs that become verified over time (credit, income, assets, property, structure), allowing mortgage pricing to become more precise and consistent.

Procedural Interpretation
Viewing outcomes as system results rather than personal judgments.

Prohibited Misuse
Any use of the Middle Credit Score® concept that creates confusion, misrepresentation, or false affiliation.

Qualifying Score
The score used by a lender to evaluate eligibility and pricing within guidelines.

Readiness
A state where understanding is sufficient to interpret information without anxiety.

Reference-Based Learning
Education focused on orientation and interpretation rather than action.

Reporting Cycle
The timing at which creditors send updates to bureaus.

Residential Mortgage Lending (National System)
A nationwide lending ecosystem operating under shared standards.

Score Spread
The range between a borrower's highest and lowest scores at a given moment.

Score Variation
Normal differences in scores caused by timing and reporting differences.

Self-Guided Education
Learning that occurs voluntarily without pressure or outcomes driving interpretation.

Signal vs. Noise
Signal refers to mortgage-relevant indicators; noise refers to visible but irrelevant changes.

Single-Score Display
The presentation of one score for simplicity in consumer tools.

Snapshot
A point-in-time view of a borrower's credit profile.

Sequence Reversal

Reordering the mortgage experience so education and interpretive context come before decisions and outcomes (education → interpretation → action).

Standard Residential Mortgage Guidelines

Mainstream underwriting frameworks used for most residential loans.

Standardization

The application of consistent rules across the lending ecosystem.

Standardized Education Framework

A shared baseline structure explaining mortgage concepts before opinion.

Stabilizing Reference Point

The middle score used to organize multiple inputs without reliance on extremes.

Structured Outcome

A result produced by an established lending framework.

Three-Bureau Score Set

A set of three credit scores pulled at the same time from three separate credit reporting organizations, used for mortgage evaluation and Middle Credit Score® identification.

Threshold

A defined reference point separating one outcome from another.

Timing (Mortgage Context)

The point when mortgage information becomes useful and measurable because the borrower has enough structure and context to interpret it correctly.

Timing Differences (Reporting Lag)

Delays between activity and bureau updates.

Transaction-Driven Information

Information delivered during active lending under emotional pressure.

Transactional Pressure

Urgency created when learning is tied to pending outcomes.

Trademark Protection (Education Context)

Protecting terminology to preserve meaning and prevent misuse.

Tri-Merge Credit Report

A mortgage credit report combining data from all three bureaus.

Underwriting Context

The principle that scores must be understood by how they are used.

Urgency

Emotion-driven pressure caused by uncertainty rather than process.

Versioning

The controlled process of maintaining and publishing official definitions over time.

Visibility Gap

When widely used systems are poorly understood because they operate quietly.

Certification Scope and Use

This publication serves as the official educational reference for the Middle Credit Score® Fundamentals Certification.

Completion of this material and successful certification indicates familiarity with standardized mortgage credit terminology, concepts, and structural frameworks as defined herein.

Certification does not confer authority to provide consumer financial advice, determine lending decisions, interpret proprietary underwriting systems, or guarantee outcomes.

This publication is intended solely as an educational standardization resource.

This edition reflects the Middle Credit Score® Fundamentals educational framework as of 3/2026.

Certification candidates are evaluated based on the standards in effect at the time of examination.